Glances at Eternity

A Memoir and More
By Glenn Maxwell

Book Cover by Peter C. Henderson

Coeditors: Diane Hussey,
              Peter C. Henderson
              and Royal Adams

DEDICATION

I dedicate this book to my beloved wife,
Sally—My Earth Angel.

Glances at Eternity

Table of Contents

ACKNOWLEDGEMENTS

I want to thank my beloved Father God for allowing me to live, as there have been many times I might have departed from this wonderful planet Earth. I also thank Him for sending me my dear, Angel Ruth, for without her I would not be sharing my experiences with you.

I want to thank Margaret Napier who has believed in my book throughout and has been unfailingly supportive while working so hard to find the right publisher for this book. She found a gentleman named Royal Adams and his wife Karen, who are also inspired by this book. I know that we are going to be friends for life. It's a wonderful collaboration.

Special thanks goes to our dear friend, Diane Hussey for listening to my pathetic attempts to get my story told with some semblance of coherence. I kept giving her rambling audiotapes—and she somehow managed to get my words down on paper in readable prose. She did a great job at a time when she was going through one of the roughest periods of her life. A thousand bouquets to you, Diane!

Next, I can't tell you how much I appreciate my brother-in-law, Pete Henderson for the hours that he put into co-editing this book without ever thinking of himself and just making it a labor of love. Then, out of the goodness of his heart, he took it upon himself to design the book's cover. He has so many talents that it boggles the mind. He is the best brother-in-law one could have and I mean it when I call him *brother*.

In this life, God has sent us three friends that are irreplaceable to us in every way you can imagine. They have become so close to us that they have become "family". They are John Dansdill, Mark Sanders and Rob Massick. We call John, St. John, because that is what he is to all that know him. John just quietly goes around taking care of all of the needs that come up to make life easier for us and his friends. He gives unconditionally and is really an Earth Angel to one and all. Our special friend, Mark has a boat and he has taken us on evening cruises where we can relax while he fixes the best foods. He has been a terrific friend and our life would be very empty without him. Rob is just a great guy. We have been on some short trips with him and have had nothing but great times.

These men are irreplaceable to us in every way you can imagine. They are our rocks on this Earth plane. *Thank you, guys—you are the best!*

New in our lives is a young woman named Katie Russell. Katie is a budding Angel artist who lives in Clinton, Ohio. Katie has an Angel named James. James is wonderful! We have spiritually adopted her as our daughter and her four children, Carrisa, Russell, Duke and Ali. They all have become our spiritually adopted grandchildren. Each of these children has their own unique spiritual gifts. They all give so much love and are so supportive to us, as we are with them. I think our relationship with this family was truly made in heaven. Thank you God for this special family in our lives.

More thanks go to two guys who have been my friends for years and years, Lou Miller and Gordie (Joe) Atkinson. Thanks guys for all the help, love and support through all those years. Have we had some laughs or what?!

I also want to acknowledge my friend, Richard Welles and his wife Patricia and their two sons, Rob and Rick, who are my Godsons, for always being there through many years of good times and bad. I love you.

Special thanks to Andy Lakey, Nick Bunick and Ali Minor and her husband Al McDaniels, Keith Richardson and his wife Francesca. These are people whose special spiritual gifts are talked about in this book and who have shared their spiritual messages with me, as I have with them. It has helped us tremendously to share these experiences with each other. It has helped to know that you are not the only one going through these spiritual experiences. Thank you to all of you for sharing and caring.

I want to thank my father and mother for raising me during the depression years with such love that I never knew I was materially poor. I want to thank my sister Althea for putting up with me as a young man and who always loved me unconditionally. Thanks to my fabulous brothers Jay, Curt, Dutch and Doug for being the best brothers anyone could ever hope to have. I also have many aunts, uncles, nieces, nephews and cousins too numerous to mention by name. I love you all dearly and was truly blessed when born into this wonderful family.

I can't leave out my sons, Dean and Reid, for loving me back so much and always being there for me. I want to thank Sally's sons, Jeff and Greg for always being so gracious to me, as they live far away from me. I want to thank Jeff's first wife, Linda for giving me the most wonderful grandchildren, Jackie, Bobby, and Cherrié, and who are for me, sadly, all grown up now, but still wonderful. I want to thank my present daughter-in-laws...Dean's wife, Darla, and Jeff's wife, Kelly for being angels to me when they see me. I also want to thank Kelly for sharing her children Amber and Jason, as my grandchildren. I'm proud of all of you.

Last but not least, I want to thank my beloved wife, Sally. Without her unfailing support, her care, her encouragement and love, this book could never have been written.

PROLOGUE

My Angel Ruth told me to write this book. She gets her orders as all Angels do, directly from Almighty God. One pays attention when one receives a suggestion from our precious Lord and one obeys!

Oh, I am a very sane person and Angel Ruth is very real. If you read this book, you will learn how and when Angel Ruth came into my life. She has informed me that this life of mine is going to get very interesting and will keep getting better in every way! I like this good news. I have been told that this change will come very "soon".

I have had time to reflect on my life since this project began and I have to admit my life fascinates me and if it fascinates me, it ought to dazzle you! One of the best parts of my life is that I am still living it. Two times I have died and two times I have come back to tell about it. When a person dies and returns to the living, it is referred to as a "near-death" experience. I've often wondered why they are called "near-death" experiences, because you really are quite dead. There is nothing "near" about it. You are gone! . . . Zappo! . . . Out of here! Like Lazarus in the Bible, you come back to life after you are *dead*. Period!

In this book you will read about the visions I see in the sky on clear nights. I also had a vision in the sky in broad daylight that was overwhelming. I shall attempt to describe them all to you, as they were (and still are) breathtaking.

Before Angel Ruth came to me, my life was far from boring. My goal in writing this memoir is not to glorify myself, but to glorify God. That is why I am only going to share the highlights of my life with you. They are important to this book because they will show you the miracles along the way and some of these miracles have been astounding. I should have been killed, or at least severely injured many times, but these things didn't happen as would be expected and on at least one occasion I was removed miraculously from the situation.

I have had "many lives" right in *this* lifetime, as I look back, I see that I have been through many different aspects of life and now I realize that I am being groomed to do God's work during the Millennium. These *many lives* I have experienced in this lifetime, were given to me so I could understand more cross-levels of society, as we know it.

I was born into a totally happy and loving family that was desperately poor during the depression years. I went through the Korean War as a Corpsman and saw brutality beyond description. I will share with you the amazing coincidences that altered my life, leading toward what most men would consider Every Man's Dream Come True, meaning that I married a very famous movie star. Through this union, I became infamous. I was around great wealth and power, mingling with the rich and famous. Some of these people were the most important people of that time. I liked them and I think they liked me.

You will read that I have been poor and happy, poor and unhappy, rich and overjoyed and also rich and miserable. I have had good health and I have been so sick that two times, as I said before, I have died and come back to life. I have been the nicest guy you could ever meet and, I am ashamed to admit there have been occasions that I have been arrogant, selfish and just plain mean.

After my first near-death experience, I started really praying prayers of gratefulness every morning and every night and I have been doing this for twenty-three years now. I became a Reiki[1] therapist (Levels I and II), quit drinking alcohol twenty-four years ago and I have led a decent, good and fun-filled life, sharing with and caring for people I love and know, but also sometimes doing the same for people I do not know. I thought with my near-death experiences that my life was different than most; but on August 18, 1997, when I saw my first vision in the night sky and again on February 25, 1998, when I first saw my dear Angel Ruth, I knew that my life was *really* unusual. It had changed forever and was headed in a direction that would become a fabulous and exciting adventure. Each day brings new surprises.

One of the wonderful benefits I've enjoyed during the experience of writing this book is being led to well known people that have had various stunning spiritual experiences and written books about those experiences. Some of these books have even been best sellers. All these books are important because these days people really do need hope. These books have to be the truth, the whole truth and nothing but

---

[1] *For those of you who are not familiar with Reiki (ray-kee), it is a universal life energy a balanced healing energy flowing directly through the therapist. Reiki works on four levels: physical, mental, emotional and spiritual. It is a very old form of Oriental healing. It is believed to have originated in Tibet, India and China (as quoted in Reiki Hands That Heal, written by my Reiki Master Teacher Joyce J. Morris, M.S., C.A.D.C.).*

the truth, for if they are not honest, God will expose them in time.

People are starved for love, decency, integrity, truth, peace and harmony. They are looking for God to make things right and fair on this planet. The good news is that everything *is* going to be made right and fair. I have been told that this will start happening "soon". As there is no time frame in Heaven, "soon" can be longer than we think; but I feel that all the good things will start happening by the beginning of the Millennium and continue for many years to come.

I receive messages all day long from Angel Ruth every single day. Sometime she even wakes me up during my sleep. Some of the messages she has relayed to me cannot be told at this time, either in this book or anywhere else. But I have been told that when the right time comes, I can write this information in another book for the entire world to read. Be patient.

Of course I am not the only person being given these messages in one form or another, and I have been told there are thousands of people being awakened. You could be one of them. You could be called to do God's work for Him in the Millennium to come. Be ready if you are called. If you are, it will leave no doubt in your mind that you have been chosen. Be prepared, because I can tell you right now that when the call comes, it is a supreme adventure!

If you choose to read this book of mine, I hope you enjoy reading it as much as I enjoyed writing it. Love, peace and light.

GLENN MAXWELL
January, 1999

INTRODUCTION

An Overview

What would happen if someone wrote a book entitled, *Life after Death* or perhaps, *What Happens After You Die?* and when you opened it there were 250 or so blank pages. On the last page it says, simply, "THE END".

Some people would say, "Just as I thought!" But most folks would be very surprised. The truth is the last page should read. THE BEGINNING".

Carl Jung had a near-death experience and this is what he had to say about it:

What happens after death is so unspeakably glorious that our imaginations and our feelings do not suffice to form even an approximate conception of it.

I have to agree with Carl Jung because I have personally had two NDE's. In this book, *Glances at Eternity*, I will take you step-by-step through the entire process of what I felt when I died, and the wonderful journey I took when my spirit left my body. I will endeavor to describe everything I saw, felt or experienced in my death process. I will include the moment I left my body, met my Guardian Angel, traveled through time and space above the planets and stars through the darkness, and then through the tunnel of light and my entrance into the Kingdom of Heaven.

Chapter One

I SHOULD HAVE BEEN DEAD

It was Saturday, November 12, 1994, three in the afternoon to be exact. I had been doing some running around town and I started to get sharp, shooting pains in my chest. Had to be indigestion, right? I would burp and the pains would stop. Then, occasionally, they returned and would stay around a little longer. Another burp and they were gone again. So I kept doing my errands. I probably should have gone to the hospital, but I thought about it and just passed it off as nothing. Pain . . . Burp . . . Pain gone. Nothing to worry about. But why did my thoughts keep returning to my wonderful Sally, my best friend, my soul mate, my wonderful wife...Sally.

Sally is a great reader of books...all types of books and magazines as well. As most of you know, about five years ago books about Angels flooded the market. Sally could not read enough about Angels! Every now and then she would make me quit watching a television show that I was completely absorbed in and make me listen to some unbelievable Angel story that happened to someone. I say unbelievable, but these tales

1

were wonderful because now I know they were true, and it was stunning what happened to the people involved. I hated being interrupted from my show, but once she got going, she had my full attention.

Anyway, on the day I felt those chest pains and was practicing my self-prescribed burp therapy, I was driving home on one of our California freeways, and the traffic was heavy. It was Saturday, early in the evening and people were hitting the road for the fun night ahead. But I was having no fun at all. The pains were really getting my attention now and I had to admit to myself that it was more than simple indigestion. Then it happened. A bomb went off in my chest. The pain was excruciating and I was afraid that I might black out. I looked over to the inside lanes as I had to get off the freeway somehow, but there was no free space between all the speeding cars. My thoughts at that time were of other people on the freeway. I did not want to pass out and injure or perhaps even kill anyone, but what was I going to do? I looked down at my speedometer and I was doing 75 mph. I had my turn signal on, but no one cared to let me out of my lane. I was totally hemmed in and could not get off that freeway.

Out of the blue I remembered something Sally had told me about Angels. She said that the Angels will always be there to help you but you have to *ask them to help you* and tell them what you need them to do. In desperation I decided to try it. I said, "Angels, I don't know if you're here with me or not, but if you are, I am asking you to please help me get home as fast as I can because I am in great pain and I'm afraid I'll pass out and kill some innocent people. Please help me!" Then I glanced toward the inside lanes and it was just miraculous. *Both lanes were empty.* This was astonishing! I immediately pulled over and was going to stop but a voice kept telling me to keep going because if I stopped I would die right there on the side of the road. So I kept going as fast as I could manage. At last the turnoff to the street I needed came up. I had six traffic lights to go before reaching home. I kept worrying about the lights because I didn't think I could stay conscious if I had to stop and wait for a red light to change. The Angels must have been worried, too, and every signal turned green as I approached it and the next thing I knew I was in front of my apartment. Now I had to walk up the fifteen steps to my door and unlock it. I managed to do it.

As I walked through the door I was all bent over and I said to Sally, "I'm very sick." She asked me if I was kidding or telling the truth.

Through clenched teeth I told her I was really sick. She rushed up to me and got my jacket off and sat me on the bed. Then she looked at my blotchy white damp face and knew instantly I was having a heart attack. She got me as comfortable as she could. I wanted to lie down, but she said that was the worst thing I could do. I was scared by now, I mean really frightened. Waves of nausea kept sweeping over me and I was sweating profusely. Adding to the searing pain in my chest, another pain had entered my jaw. Could I make it to the hospital in time? I didn't think so.

Now I managed to tell Sally how much my jaw was hurting and she immediately put her hands on both sides of my face and performed Reiki on me. As I've mentioned, both of us are Reiki Level I and Level II therapists. The moment she touched my jaw my eyes flew open in amazement as the pain immediately left me. When Sally was finally able to dial 911 I heard her tell whoever answered that she would be waiting out on the balcony to show the Emergency Medical Technicians (EMT's) where we were. She opened the front door but felt she had to come back to my side to see how I was doing. I don't think she was with me for thirty seconds when the medical team walked through the open door. Sally asked, "How in the world did you get here so fast?" They said they were only a block away and were getting ready to go back to the hospital when they got the call for assistance. Coincidence? I prefer to see it as a miracle. Thank You, God!

The EMT's immediately hooked me up to a heart monitor and gave me oxygen, which helped my breathing. Then they strapped me onto a gurney and rolled me into the ambulance, gently loading me into the rear compartment. Sally sat up front with the driver. The driver did not turn on the siren or go over 55 mph, so neither Sally or I thought my condition was really all that serious. It was only this year that Sally read that a very serious heart patient must be driven slowly to the hospital, with no siren, as speed and a siren would over-stimulate the patient's heart. So, in this case, ignorance was bliss. I thank Father God for sending the perfect ambulance driver who was aware of this information and adhered to it.

As there was no barrier between the front and back of the ambulance, Sally would call back every once in awhile, "How are you doing, Honey?" I'd tell her I was doing fine. It took twenty minutes to reach the emergency room from our apartment. As I was being transferred from the ambulance to the hospital I mentioned that the pain was much, much better. The

EMT's then asked how much I was hurting on a scale of 1 to 10. I thought about this and then said, "Hmm . . . maybe a 2."

Sally was told to go to the waiting room and call back to the emergency room in about forty minutes. On her way to the waiting room she asked the lady EMT who had been monitoring my heartbeat with a small scanner if there was anything showing up on it. The lady EMT got a very sad look on her face and stuck out her lower lip and shook her head up and down indicating, "Yes." Sally thought this was odd because I was cheerful by now and telling this EMT lady what an angel she was. I was just being my usual euphoric self. Sally thought I'd had a slight heart attack and they would send me home and tell me to change my diet and stop smoking. She waited the forty minutes and then called the emergency room. She was informed that I was getting ready to be sent upstairs. They expressed their surprise that no one had come out and spoken to her about my condition and what they were planning to do about it. They said someone would be out immediately and talk to her about my case.

* * *

I'll get back to Sally, but this is what happened to me. The doctors ran tests and found that I had suffered a coronary thrombosis. A blood clot had entered and stuck in the center of my heart and then moved, and damaged the outside of my left ventricle and proceeded to enter the inside of that ventricle and do some damage there, too. In short, *I should have been dead!* When they told me this, I thought of my Dad because this was the exactly the same thing that killed him.

The emergency room nurses asked what time the attack occurred and decided that the time frame was perfect for a T.P.A. treatment. This process dissolves all the blood clots anywhere in your body. Please take care of yourselves, all of you who are reading this. The procedure saved my life but was painful beyond description. The doctors injected something into my bloodstream to dissolve the bad stuff. The medical staff had their gallows humor in high gear and referred to this treatment as giving their patient the "Roto-Rooter". Actually, this very accurately describes the procedure. I now feel sorry for plugged toilets and sinks. Just kidding! But this awful yet wonderful treatment saved my life at least for the moment. One interesting note. Despite everything that followed I have never had any pain in my heart again from that day to this. Thank You, Father God and Your Holy Angels.

* * *

After the horrible T.P.A. treatment I was still alive and kicking and being prepared to be taken upstairs to Intensive Care. Meanwhile, a very pretty young woman who introduced herself as my doctor walked up to Sally in the waiting room. Sally was surprised that this woman was a doctor because she looked so young. Sally asked about my status and the young doctor said that my condition was critical. Sally was shocked and said, "Critical as in DIE?" The doctor nodded yes. Sally then said, "Are you trying to tell me you don't expect him to live through the night?" With a sad expression the doctor again nodded, "I'm sorry."

Sally says she knows it sounds insane, but she just wanted to laugh hysterically at the idea of me being dead. She couldn't imagine anyone as wonderful as me (her words), a person who lights up a room with his smile, who helps so many people with kind words and is so cheerful all the time, could die. She knew if she laughed, the doctor would think she was nuts. So she simply thanked the nice doctor for her honesty and held back her almost uncontrollable urge to break up laughing. Finally the doctor told her that she could see me in about an hour and that I could be found on the 6th floor in the Intensive Care Unit. Sally said a great calm came over her. She could hardly move, but she went to a pay phone and the first call she made was to our Reiki family who does absentee healing. This is sending healing energy and they told her they would immediately start sending this energy to both of us. She then phoned the Ministry of Prayer and asked them to pray for me. Then she called my brother, Dutch, with the bad news and he rushed to the hospital to be with me.

When Dutch arrived he was his usual cool, calm self at least on the outside, but inside he was Jell-O. Sally and my brother went upstairs to wait apprehensively for some change in my condition. Only my wife was allowed into my room. As she walked in I was sitting up in bed chatting merrily away with no less than five doctors and several nurses in attendance. I was hooked up like a cow to a milking machine with all sorts of lines leading from my chest, fingers and arms to various medical devices. One of the doctors came up to Sally and asked her if she had any questions. Sally said she did and asked if I would have to have open-heart surgery. He looked at her as if she might be off her rocker and said, "Heavens no!" Well, she thought that was encouraging. She came up to me and said, "I love you and I'll pray for you." Instead of giving her my usual wonderful smile, I yelled at her, saying, "Why are you always talking?" She actually apologized only to be yelled at again, "See? You're always talking. Just shut up!" That's when one of the physicians became alarmed and said, "Here, here! We'll have none of that." Sally didn't want to upset me any more so she just moved away from me. Now you have to remember that the doctor told Sally that they did not expect me to live through the night. She looked over at the heart monitor machine and the display was bouncing around like a wild Ping-Pong game. Instinctively she knew this was not good.

With Sally standing there in a muted state one of the doctors started talking about the big football game that was being played the next day and asked me who I was betting on. I told him who I thought was going to win and the doctor agreed with me. Then he said that I could look forward to watching the game. As the game was being played the next day this was an encouraging comment. I might have at least 24 more hours!

My wife didn't know what to make of this at all. She had just been told that I probably wouldn't last the night. She was thinking, "What? Watch a football game?" She couldn't understand how they could even suggest that I watch football. Even if I lived through the night, the excitement of the game (I am a passionate fan) could *kill* me. This greatly disturbed Sally.

Eventually, all the medical people left except one truly extraordinary nurse. The doctors had left my room with big smiles about the upcoming football contest. I was smiling too, sitting up in bed all jazzed up about seeing that big game.

The remaining nurse looked absolutely gorgeous, just what you would expect an Earth Angel (my term for extraordinarily kind and helpful people I have encountered in my life) to look like with her blue-gray eyes, no make-up, and honey blonde hair worn shoulder length; she also had a piercing intelligence. It turned out that she was the best cardiac specialist nurse you could ever hope for. Not only that, she was also kind and compassionate. Sally was thinking about me watching the football game. She was thinking, "Maybe the first diagnosis that Glenn won't live through the night is wrong. Oh, please, God, make it so." But when she asked the nurse (out of my hearing), she got the same sad face, lower lip stuck out, that she had received before. Apparently, I was hopeless. Sally looked her right in the eye and said, "No! He's going to make it!" The nurse said, "But . ." and Sally stopped her immediately and said,

11

"No buts. He is . . . going . . . to . . . make it," staring right into the nurse's eyes and not backing down. After what might have been a half a minute the nurse finally nodded, "I believe you." Sally then told the nurse that she would be calling every two hours and expected good news—each and every time she called. The nurse said that if I did make it through that night that I would live. By this time it was late in the evening and Sally left with Dutch, knowing that I was in very competent hands.

Sally wanted to be alone to make calls to my family, her family and to our very close friends. She asked for their prayers and everyone said that we would get them. She knew that was true, too. Then she started her own prayers and began sending healing Reiki energy. During this time she received a message from heaven. She wrote it down:

Do you need me? I am here. Do not be concerned. All will be taken care of. Now you cannot see my way, but you will see it soon. All else will be added unto you.

Sally doesn't know how to drive. She just knew that the phrase "all would be taken care of" meant that she would always have a ride to the hospital any time of the day or night and sure enough, our guardian Earth Angel, John, who is our dear neighbor, took care of this. Sally also knew that I would have the best medical care and I got this, too. Thank You again, God.

Not until recently, have I finally understood what was meant by, "*Now you cannot see my way, but you will see it soon.*" It took four years, but now I know God saved me to do all the work he has for me during the Millennium. Additionally, the part that said, "*All else will be added unto you*", meant that all our needs would be met . . . financial, physical and spiritual . . . and they have been. Thank you, praise you, and we glorify our God. Amen.

After a long prayer, Sally looked up at my picture she keeps on top of the bookcase. I was smiling (of course) and she said it seemed to radiate a million beams of sunshine. It filled her with joy. Then she went to the photo albums and it seemed that every picture affected her the same way. She was very comforted by this and then she started thinking of all the years we had together and it came to her that there wasn't one word that had not been said at the proper moment. There was not a single regret. Our lives had been so full and filled with so much love and now God was revealing to her that it was a clean slate. Sally told God that if our time together on Earth were finished she would know it was "finished in beauty." She then prayed again and sent more Reiki energy and then phoned the hospital. The nurse said the minute Sally had left the room my heart had stabilized. *This was a miracle! A true honest to God miracle had happened...I should not have lived!*

Sally fell asleep around two in the morning and then had awakened only to feel death and evil close by. She was very afraid. She shouted out loud to Satan in no uncertain terms. She said, "Satan! Stand behind me! You are *not* to be in my home or with Glenn. Get out of here and get out of here *now!*" She literally punched out in all directions with her arms and kicked each corner of the room. Then she got a broom, opened the front door and swept Satan out of the house. She knew it was probably a silly thing to do, but it made her feel better and she was then able to resume praying and sending healing Reiki energy. The Bible tells us to pray unceasingly and she was doing just that.

She had phoned the nurse a few times during the night and I was still alive. Now it was 5:30am and the nurse was euphoric. She reported, "He's cookin'! He's cruisin'! *He made it!* Of course my Sally was overjoyed. Oh, thank you, thank you, my beloved Father God!

* * *

After Sally left me to go home, the nurse came into my room. She took my temperature, pulse and respiration. She fluffed my pillow, dimmed the lights and walked out. After awhile, a strange, unfamiliar feeling swept over my whole body. It didn't take long too long for me to recognize what it was. It was fear. For the first time I realized that I was really scared. I didn't want to die but had been told by almost everyone I'd talked to that there was a good chance that I would not make it through the night…that I would never see another sunrise or sunset. Oh, yes . . . Glenn Maxwell was terrified.

Everything had become very quiet. All I could see through the drape that was pulled around my bed was the silhouette of a nurse going past the open door. I was alone with my thoughts now, and I had never felt more alone in my entire lifetime. Sure, I could hear my heart beating and I knew that I was breathing, but . . . for how long? I knew there was no way that I was going to sleep that night. No way at all.

I began to review my life. I decided to go back as far as I could remember and look into my past to see if I had lived it well or just wasted the time. My thoughts went first back to my childhood and my beloved family I loved so much . . .

Chapter-Two

ONE VERY CLOSE FAMILY

Now here is something that is pretty neat! The whole world celebrates my birthday every single year! You see, I was born on New Year's Eve. Actually, it was in the afternoon at 12:10 p.m., December 31, 1931.

My nine-and-a-half year old sister, Althea, nicknamed "Sissy", was not pleased that I was the fourth boy born in a row. She wanted a little sister. She told the doctor in no uncertain terms to just send me back where I came from. The doctor said shortly that this wasn't possible and that she just had to accept me. I guess I was a cheerful and happy little guy and she grew to love me dearly, taking such good care of me that I was three years old before I came to realize she wasn't my mother!

Mom was always busy with household chores and cooking for her large family. There were no shortcuts in those days before our modern conveniences. My sister was put pretty much in charge of her four brothers. She made us mind in no uncertain terms. My brothers and I look up to her to this day.

I was raised in a small town in Northern California. The town is located in the foothills of the great Sierra Nevada Mountains and is a beautiful place for a boy to run free and communicate with nature. It's a place where there are lakes blue and deep, and rivers running wild. There are animals and fish and beauty just everywhere. It rained and snowed in the winter and the sun shone warm and bright in the summer. In my family, there were Mom and Dad, my sister Althea, and my three brothers, Jay, Curt and Dutch. I was the youngest or what's called "the baby of the family." At least I was until thirteen years later when my brother, Doug, came along. He was the fifth boy and the last child to be born to my parents. So Sissy never got herself a little sister, but by then Sissy was all grown up.

Every day my Dad and two oldest brothers would go hunting. Brother Dutch and I would fish and work in the vegetable garden. I don't ever remember going hungry or doing without a thing. I was the happiest kid in the world. I had it all.

I can't even count the many animals in the forest and fish in the streams that gave their lives so that my family and I could sustain our own existences. To those creatures I give my humble thanks.

Anyone who can remember the Depression knows how hard life was then. There was no real money anywhere in town, but in a way that was a wonderful thing as it pretty much made everyone equal. If you wanted to be respected you earned that respect by being compassionate and sharing with others and helping each other along the way. What a shame that this way of life, this priceless lesson, is becoming increasingly rare.

I always felt so lucky to be raised in my beautiful town. Not only did we have the fish and game and lakes and streams, there was also wild fruit and berries all through the foothills. Mom made the greatest blackberry cobbler you've ever wrapped your lips around and since the berries grew wild everywhere, they were free. What bounty!

You might say we were poor, but what we didn't have in material goods we made up for with love, laughter, music and adventure. God, I couldn't wait to get up in the morning and start each new day. My family was full of joy and I guess it showed in the way we loved each other, supported each other and pretty much stuck together.

There were no refrigerators in those days although some folks had iceboxes. We couldn't afford the ice and it was difficult to keep anything fresh for very long. So, when Dad, Jay and Curt would come home from the hunting party, we always would keep what we wanted, then Dad would give anything extra to the neighbors. Nothing was ever wasted, and you can't imagine the happiness it brought to these people when he dropped off meat for their families.

My real heroes were my Mom, Dad, sister and older brothers. They were my Captain Marvel, Superman, Dick Tracy, Batman and Wonder Woman all rolled up together. And I was always so proud when they would take time to help me with a problem or try to teach me things that they knew but were mysteries to me. I would try so hard to make them proud of me and even if I didn't always succeed, I was always trying.

My Dad was the hardest-working man I ever knew. I can't remember any time that he wasn't working. He and my cousin Pete started a small lumber mill. They would take a big tree and cut it into 2x4's, 4x8's and planks for the railroad. That must have been hard labor, wrestling with that green timber.

Everyone loved my Dad. He always had a kind word to say about everyone. He was quick to smile and loved to laugh. He also loved hearing jokes and repeating them. He loved to sing and dance, play cards and enjoyed having a drink now and then.

I remember those guys working their brains out Monday through Friday, then Saturday would roll around and they would party all night. Right after dinner all the furniture would be carried outside to make room for everyone to dance. Some of our neighbors were musical and they showed up every week. I remember a fiddler, guitar player, bass man and an accordionist. Never a man to be left out, my Dad contributed to the music by twanging on what he called his "Jew's Harp".

How the grownups could party! They would break out the home brew and white lightning for the guys and maybe a little sedate homemade wine for the ladies. The music would start right after dinner and the dancing would go on until the early hours of the morning. Us kids were all sent upstairs where blankets were laid out for us to fall asleep on when we got tired. It was fun for everyone.

It amuses me now to think about my Dad playing his Jew's Harp. As a small child I never saw that little sucker because Dad's big hands completely hid it when he played. I thought he was playing his teeth! When I was about five I decided to give this a try. I stood on a chair in front of the bathroom mirror and cupped my little hands up to my mouth. I was so surprised that no noise came as I plucked at my teeth. No matter how hard or how many ways I tried, no noise came from my teeth or my mouth. Many years went by before I figured out what Dad was doing to get the music to come out. I was one disappointed little kid that day. Kids! They are so precious.

Dad was not a religious man. He did believe in God and believed in all the right things, but not in going to church. He'd always say, "My church is under any tree I choose to make my church. You don't have to pray in a special building." And he never did force his children to go to church, either.

Mom was different than Dad. On Sunday, Mom would always get up early, get dressed, get me dressed and drag me off to church with her. But you know something? I learned to like going with her but probably for all the wrong reasons. You see, it gave me the whole day to rack up a lot of "points" with Mom. Kids are always competing for the love of their parents and I felt this really put me ahead. After church, I would go to Sunday school. I loved the old Bible stories about Noah and his ark, Moses parting the Red Sea and all that stuff. I don't know where the other kids in my family would disappear to during Sunday school, but they sure had good hideouts! So, I guess I was about six years old when I got my first introduction to God and Angels and I was a real believer.

My first two miracles came very early in my life. I remember when I was about 7 or 8 years old that I prayed for a BB gun for Christmas. I wanted that gun so badly and would pray for it every night. I think my Dad must have heard me. On Christmas morning we could hardly wait to open up our presents. Mom passed them all out to us and when I ripped the paper off my present, sure as shootin', there it was, a beautiful, shiny new BB gun complete with a tube of BB's. To the young me this really was a miracle. I mean, where did they get the money? *Wow!* It was beginning to snow but I couldn't wait to go outside and try out my new artillery. I put on my coat and boots and went out into the crisp, snowy outside air, bravely clutching the gun, feeling like Davy Crockett or Daniel Boone. I imagined I'd surely come back with a plump wild turkey for Christmas dinner, but it was so cold I stayed near the house.

It was snowing harder now and I should have gone back in but I didn't want to return before christening my gun with at least one shot. I looked up and down the road for a suitable target and way down the road I saw the wires carrying electricity to the town. Sitting on those wires was a group of about ten fat blackbirds. With the skill and cunning of a cat, the fearless hunter sneaked up on those innocent birds. When I was in range I raised the BB gun to my shoulder, took careful aim, took a deep breath and let it out, slowly squeezing the trigger just the way Dad had taught me. By this time there must have been about eight inches of snow on the ground. I felt the recoil as the gun fired and the bird I was aiming at fell from the wire and I watched, now horrified, as its helpless little body tumbled into the snow. I dropped the gun and ran to the place where it had fallen.

When I saw the bird lying in the snow, still as death, I got sick to my stomach and started crying uncontrollably. I picked that bird up and held it to my chest to keep it warm. Between sobs and tears I told the bird how sorry I was and begged it, "Please don't die." I put it back in the snow and remembered that only God can create a miracle, so I fell to my knees and began to pray. "Please Father God, don't let him die." I was so sorry that I had shot it. But nothing happened. The bird just lay there. Mom was calling me from the house so I picked up my gun, brushing the snow from it and started back. For some reason, as I was leaving, I walked over to have one more look at the dead bird. Just as I got there I got my second miracle of the day. The bird wobbled to its feet, shook its feathers and took off flying! I thanked God for this wonderful miracle and promised that I would never again kill for the pure enjoyment of killing and to this day I have kept that promise.

***

I remember waking up one beautiful Sunday morning to find everyone else in the house huddled around the radio. I looked at Mom and Sis and tears were streaming from their eyes. My Dad and older brothers were unusually quiet. "What's going on? What is it?" I kept asking but no one would pay any attention to me. They just told me to hush up and be quiet. I heard a man on the radio say that the Japanese had pulled a sneak attack at a place called Pearl Harbor. The Japanese had destroyed most of the ships of the United States Navy and hundreds of American sailors were killed.

My Dad was furious and called the Japanese every filthy name in his vocabulary. The air was blue from his cursing. I'd heard Dad curse before when he was angry, but Mom would always scold him and say, "Jim! Not in front of the children." But on this day she was still. It seemed like hours had gone by and President Franklin Delano Roosevelt made his famous speech about that "Day of Infamy", Sunday, December 7, 1941.

I'll never forget that speech. In essence, the President said that we were at war with Japan, Germany and Italy. He said that all able-bodied men were to report to their draft boards or to their nearest recruiting stations. And I'll never forget the next few moments of utter stillness, my Dad looking at Jay and Curt and the way Curt and Jay's eyes met and just locked on each other as if they were communicating without saying a word. I left the room and got my BB gun. I was ready to go to war . . . whatever that was.

The next day was Monday and somehow we all ended up in town. I remember seeing men lined up and joining up for the war. It looked like every man in the whole county was trying to get in any branch of the service they could. My oldest brother Jay ended up in the Army and became a paratrooper in the 101st Airborne Division. My next to oldest brother Curtis joined the Navy and became a SeaBee in the South Pacific. Jay was sent to Europe to fight the Nazis and Curt would be fighting the "Japs" as we had started calling them. My Dad wanted to go, but he knew he couldn't because he still had a family to care for. Although my sister Althea couldn't fight with the boys, she later married a young lieutenant from our hometown. Her husband, Phillip Reeg went on to become a major and was stationed in India.

The days, weeks, months and years that followed were long and wearisome. It was a tough time for me, too. Most of my heroes were gone and in harm's way and I was frightened and worried for them. I prayed for their safety every night as only a little boy can pray and each morning I would trudge off dutifully for school. That was all Dutch and I could do...go to school and try not to bother Mom and Dad.

The summer of 1942 we moved to Concord, California. Dad got a job at the shipyards in Richmond and built ships for the war effort. I graduated from Jr. High and went into High School. Somewhere in that first or second year of High School I became interested in medicine. I was obsessed with anything to do with medicine or surgery. I couldn't walk away from any book or article about the anatomy of the human body and what made it work. Don't get me wrong, I did have my hot rod and girl phase like most every other guy, but hidden in my soul was a deep love and respect for the art and science of medicine.

One day I came home from school and found my Dad holding my Mom in is arms. They were both crying. I looked on the kitchen table and there was the telegram from the War Department notifying us that their beloved son Jay was missing in action. He was in combat at the Battle of the Bulge in Belgium. I went in my bedroom and didn't come out. One of my heroes was missing and probably dead so very far from home and they couldn't even find his body. I cried and cried but that wasn't doing any good.

That night I said my prayers as never before. I explained to God that Jay didn't want to be over there fighting this war. We didn't want him to have to be there. I prayed to God, "If you have the power that we believe you do have, please find my brother and send him home." About a week later another telegram arrived informing us that Jay was alive and had been found recuperating in a hospital. He was going to be just fine. Oh, Father God, thank you so very much! Now after that incident I was a firm believer in God and his Angels and everything I ever read about God and His miracles. How could I not believe?

The war in Europe slowly ground down and came to an end and Jay finally got to come home. But the war with Japan was still hot and I had another hero to get home. When the United States dropped two A-bombs that totally destroyed two of Japan's largest cities the war ended just like that. Curt finally made it back to us, safe and sound.

Chapter Three

MY DAD

At last, at last the war was over and after seeing the slaughter and the waste of so much of the world's greatest resource, it's young men, I will always believe that war has to be man's greatest stupidity. But at last things were pretty much back to normal and the whole family was at home and at peace. I finished my sophomore year of High School and was looking forward to that summer vacation of 1948, which I spent swimming and really just basically goofing until one hot, awful mid-summer day.

On the sixth of August I came home to find a line of company pickups and cars in the street in front of our house. I knew something terrible had happened and I didn't even want to go in but I had to. As I walked in I saw my mother crying surrounded by a lot of people I didn't know. My dear, beloved Dad had died that morning.

He had gone to work and someone told him a joke. Just as he started to burst out laughing he suffered a massive heart attack and was dead before he hit the ground. Reflecting on this now, it must have been a fine way to go out. No suffering, just a big laugh, that left his face with a great big smile in death. God bless his blessed soul. Such a kind and decent man. It was a terrible day. It was a terrible day for the whole *world* as far as I was concerned. We tried to settle Mom down, but there was nothing we could say or do except just try to be there for her because the tears would still be coming long after Dad's death.

* * *

Before going on, I would like to tell you of a profound, stunning spiritual experience my Dad had one year before he died.

Dad's name was Jim Maxwell. He had walked into town from our home with a young man named, Charlie Peacock. Charlie was almost like a member of our family as he was at our house so often.

While in town, Dad and Charlie had stopped at a bar on the way home to have a drink. It was in the afternoon. After one drink, they started to walk home. It was still in the afternoon and they were walking through an open field on the way to our house. Without any warning my Dad found himself flat on his back. A sudden, giant, invisible force had shoved him down.

Dad stared up, stunned at what had just happened to him and was further shocked to see Jesus Christ hovering over him. Then Jesus said, "You are my child. Give me your hand." Dad held out his hand and Jesus took it and pulled him to his feet. After Dad was standing, Jesus said, "Follow Me." and then Jesus went up into the clouds and disappeared. This left my Dad standing next to Charlie Peacock in the open field. Then my Dad dissolved into tears.

Charlie Peacock had not seen Jesus, but witnessed my Dad being slammed to the ground. Then extend his hand to get to his feet in a very strange way, an impossible way. Dad had gotten to his feet as though someone had *pulled* him up.

My Dad was finally able to gather his wits about him and was able to walk and he and Charlie managed to make it back to our house. Once home, Dad sat down and started to cry again, sobbing, and managed to tell the family that he would let them know what had happened when he could collect himself well enough to talk. But it was many hours before he could relate what had happened to him.

Charlie Peacock said he had seen the whole thing — how Dad had been slammed to earth and how he extended his hand so that he had been literally pulled to his feet by someone invisible to Charlie. He said it was the darndest thing he'd seen in his whole life.

Dad was fifty-three years old when he died. If you ever saw the movie, *Spencer's Mountain*, the Dad in that story as played by Henry Fonda was just like mine, a wonderful, wonderful man.

* * *

Something happened to me after Dad's death. I don't know what it was, but it was completely mental. I was a pretty good student up to that point and I was trying to do everything the right way. But now I started hanging around with the wrong kids. I became the leader of a gang and was getting into a lot of trouble. Not big trouble like so many of the kids today, but enough trouble that the police knew my face and knew that there was trouble afoot and something bad might happen. Somehow word got to my sister who was living in Placerville, California at the time. She thought I was "going to Hell in a hand basket" and she thought I should come live with her before I ended up in prison. You know something? She was right. Most of the gang members I was running around with that summer ended up in jail or worse.

I enjoyed living with my sister and brother-in-law, Phillip. He was great. He would sit down and talk to me and explain things to me. He wanted to know what my dreams were and he guided me toward those dreams. He was a wonderful person. He had a business going and I felt that I should help out by working with him to make up for my room and board. He let me do that and it worked out well. In fact it was a great arrangement and his business prospered and I was doing just fine in school.

Chapter Four

MY WAR, KOREA

I graduated from High School in June of 1950 and was looking forward to going to college, but a larger event intervened. The North Koreans had invaded South Korea. The United States was extremely anti-Communist and President Truman felt we had to help the South. Again the nation's youth was sent to war. But this time I was one of them. Both Dutch and I were ripe to go. Not too many guys were rushing to volunteer for this one but there was still a Draft Board and our numbers were right on top. It looked like my college career was dead in its tracks, shot down like a Communist MIG fighter plane.

I went into the United States Navy and was sent to boot camp in San Diego. After learning the basics of life in the navy I took a test and because of my interest in medicine I was accepted into the U.S. Navy Medical School. I was sent to Balboa Navy Medical Center at the Balboa Naval Hospital right there in San Diego. Out of a group of 65 students I graduated in the top five of my class with honors. Shortly after that I was given my orders to board the navy hospital ship *U.S.S. Haven* for duty in the Orient and Korea. By September 1950 I was in the Pusan perimeter where I got my first taste of war. It was not pleasant.

So there I was in Pusan, Korea. We sailed in on a bleak night and docked. The next morning I went up on deck and knew immediately that I wasn't going to like this place. The weather was freezing cold, especially for a California boy and it smelled rank and there was a helluva war going on. I thought to myself, "What in the world am I doing here?"

Our hospital beds at this time were empty but it didn't take long to fill them up. On the second day we were there, patients started arriving by helicopter. The casualties were classified either A, B or C. As the 'copters were en route to the ship they would radio us saying they had maybe five or six Class A patients which meant extremely critical wounds to the head or stomach, what we termed "long wounds." Sometimes the medical choppers would report combinations of wounds . . . say eight class B patients which meant critical but not extreme trauma, and 11 class C guys who were ambulatory. As the helicopters arrived with their pitiful cargoes, the different classes of the wounded would be separated on the flight deck and sent to either the operating room, pre-op or wherever else their wounds could be treated. We had an orthopedic unit, another unit exclusively for internal trauma, a neurosurgery unit and so on.

As I looked out from the deck of the hospital ship that first day we were in business I saw the most amazing thing. As I peered into the sky it was like seeing hundreds of dragonflies all hovering to get on one sunflower. Of course we were the sunflower and the choppers the dragonflies. For the first three or four days everyone on the ship worked a minimum of 20 hours every day. There was just no let-up. The casualties kept coming and coming …and coming. Doctors were operating 14 hours at a stretch without stopping, never leaving the operating theater. In less than a week every bed was filled, the operating rooms were full and patients in litters were lined up in most of the hallways. It wasn't a pretty sight. Some of those young marines and soldiers and South Korean troops were brought to us with missing arms and legs, some with gaping holes in their bodies, some just totally torn apart.

Our job was to function as the first stop in the recovery process meaning the quickest possible attention to all wounds. We would take the patients aboard and give them whatever surgery they needed and when they were well enough to be moved they would be airlifted to one of the real hospitals in Japan. We sent those patched up guys out night and day. The air transports would leave their airbase in Korea with their navy wounded and fly into Yokosuka Naval Hospital in Japan. The army grunts were taken to Tachakawa Army Hospital, also in Japan. This grueling schedule did not let up for more than 10 months. It was endless but at least no one ever complained about being bored. The ship's doctors and crew worked around the clock almost in an automatic state, a zombie mode, and there here was no time at all for anything resembling fun.

On the ship I met a doctor that I became fond of, perhaps the nicest person I ever met. He was always anxious to help me with any question I had regarding medicine. I believe he was a professor of medicine at the University of Chicago when he was called to war. His name was Dr. Jonathon Hart. One day we were having a cup of coffee together in the canteen when the routine summons calling everyone to the flight deck barked from the loudspeaker. Dr. Hart was at one end of the flight deck and I was at the other waiting for the choppers to land. The routine was to wait for the 'copter blades to stop, go in and get the patients off the birds and take them to the appropriate surgery. The day became more horrible than usual when all of a sudden I felt something wet and warm on the side of my face. Then something bumped against my leg and I looked down. It was Doctor Hart. Or rather it was Doctor Hart's head. Oh, God! I found out later that he had walked into one of the helicopter blades. His loss was a blow to all of us, his naval family and to his real family and the patients on board and the navy itself. He was one of those special physicians who really cares, who has compassion and will always take time to hear your problems. Because he knew I wanted to go to medical school to become a doctor he always gave me his time, the time he should have spent resting, teaching me and guiding me. I've always felt guilty about this because I know it was great fatigue that caused him to walk into that rotor to his death. It was just awful.

Back in the present, I have just made a decision. I won't turn this book into a war story although I have plenty of them. I spent four years in that place and I also spent time in the Marine Corps. I spent too many years watching the waste and stupidity of war, too much time watching man's inhumanity to man. I've seen too many men have their lives just thrown away. So, I'm not going to write any more about those things that I have spent years of my life just trying to forget.

Chapter Five

NO ONE IS PERFCT

Let's fast forward to August, 1954. A truce has been signed in Korea. Everyone there is happy we're finally going home. It's over, thank God. The only good thing to come out of that miserable time is that I gained a lot of knowledge about all phases of emergency medicine and the opportunity to work with some of the most wonderful doctors in the world. I am grateful for that.

When I got back to the States new orders were waiting for me. I was to report to Treasure Island in San Francisco and wait for my discharge. I had three or four months of duty left on my tour and during those months I just had fun, making up for all those years of horror and waste. My family lived only 25 miles from San Francisco in Concord and it was great to be home with them again and to see my brother Dutch who had made it through the war as part of the Air Force. Strangely enough although we were both in Korea for four years we never ran into each other. But I'll bet he was over there watching my back just the same as he always did from the day I was born.

For the next six weeks or so it was just party, party and more party. I was really enjoying going out every night to dance and drink, getting home in the early hours of the morning. But eventually this party life got a little boring and I was getting itchy feet.

One day as I was sitting in the emergency room at Treasure Island Naval Base. Word came down that a corpsman was needed badly and *right now*, to make one quick trip to Japan and then into Korea to pick up some of the last troops that hadn't made it home yet. I figured I wasn't doing anything all that exciting and decided to go back one more time. This turned out to be the only time I ever had fun while working in the Navy. I had a ball.

I won't give you the name of the ship, the date we sailed or any other information about the assignment. You see I might still get into a bit of trouble for some of the things I got into during that time. After being piped aboard I found that I was assigned to be in total charge of all the alcohol and drugs on board plus the ship's pharmacy and laboratory.

My first task was to take inventory. This was necessary before leaving port to make sure I had all the right equipment and the current drugs. Anything might happen aboard a ship at sea and I had to be prepared for it. As I made my inventory I checked the alcohol locker and discovered about five gallons of pure grain alcohol stored there that was never listed in any of the books. That meant only one thing. It was mine! Now, I enjoyed my cocktails at this time, but didn't plan to waste this bounty on myself. The fox had entered the hen house.

That night I pondered on how I could best use this newfound booty. On board there were only about twelve actual navy men. The rest of the personnel consisted of merchant marines. I knew that there is no alcohol allowed aboard any U.S. Navy ships and *that* suggested a plan. I got on the intercom to the head cook and asked him to meet me in the pharmacy. During this meeting we struck a little deal. I told him to order 100 crates of oranges before we sailed and if necessary to pick up more when we arrived at Yokosuka, Japan. My plan was to pass the word around the ship, a little advertising so to speak, and after we were at sea for three days I would inject one cubic centimeter of 190 proof alcohol into each orange and sell them to the merchant marines for a buck per orange. Well! You have never seen such a booming business as I had. Those merchant marines were lining up for what seemed to be miles. In fact, I had to break up the line into smaller ones so no one would know what they were lining up for. If an officer found out what I was up to it would have been big time trouble for me. Meanwhile, I was selling oranges right and left. The whole hundred crates were sold out before we reached Japan and I was looking forward to getting more oranges in Japan. With pockets bulging with money and a smiling face I looked toward the Land of the Rising Sun.

Then one morning around ten, a call rang out from the loud speaker or "bitch box" as we called it in the Navy. "Corpsman Maxwell, please report to the Captain on the bridge." Gulp! I thought, "Oh man, someone squealed on me and I'll be doing the last months of my Navy career in the brig." Time to think fast. I made my way as slowly as possible up to the bridge. (We had a nickname for this captain. We called him Hurricane Telly because he'd put that ship on full bore and he would never slow down. He broke six deck plates on a ship once in rough seas taking the great northern route from San Francisco up to Alaska which was the same route we were taking to Japan.) Now I found myself standing a bit weak in the knees in front of old Hurricane and he said, "Hey, Doc. I've noticed that all the crewmen are eating oranges. What's going on?" He had already asked the cook about it and had been politely referred straight to me. Great, now I'm supposed to tell him why the crew can't get enough oranges. "Well, it's a preventative thing, Sir." "Would you mind explaining that, corpsman?" "Not at all, Sir. I was reading the report on the ships last voyage and it said that 72% of your crew was down with influenza and colds and you had three pneumonia cases. Well, Sir, that is not going to happen on *this* trip, Sir. I'm gonna need every bunk in that hospital room and I don't want some crew guy taking up a bunk with the flu when I have a real emergency and really need that bed. So I'm pushing vitamin C on the crew as hard as I can, especially in this kind of weather." He looked at me, somewhat bemused, then smiled, patted me on the back and said, "Good thinking, Doc. Now that's good preventative medicine." "Thank you, Sir." I was home free! Thank you, Angels.

I honestly never felt badly about taking those guys money and I'll tell you why. There were only twelve Navy personnel on that ship. All the rest were civilian merchant marines making big bucks while we were getting lousy Navy pay. It was only justice.

Time can pass pretty slowly on a ship but eventually we reached Japan and we were scheduled for three stops, Yokosuka, Kobe and Sasebo. Eventually we were to cross the Yellow

Sea to Inchon, Korea to pick up our troops and return them home.

While in Japan there was an adventure or two. During the fifties just about every third building was a house of ill repute. These merchant seamen with their pockets full of money would break down all barriers to get to these places along the way. I figured that since we had three stops in Japan that this might be another good opportunity to fill up my money belt. But I had to be really cool going about it.

After we left Sasebo which was our last port-of-call in Japan, we headed for Inchon which took about a week at sea. The first part of my new plan called for a "short arm inspection" which is, to be polite, a visual check in the appropriate area for venereal disease. It was no problem to arrange a surprise inspection because I had the authority to call one. I had these swabbies down in the galley lined up in about ten lines, each line about eighty feet long, and began the inspection. Everyone went through the same procedure. After the visual examination a smear was taken. A crewman would take the smears to the lab to run the necessary tests. Now you must understand that every one of these merchant marines waiting in line had the same story that they had never been to any house of ill repute in their lives. Yeah, they were all little angels. I wouldn't say anything, just take the smear and send them on their various ways.

And how would an enterprising young corpsman make an honest dollar out of this? It wasn't too hard and it wasn't blackmail. I would call a crewman into my office and give him a form to fill out. The form was to notify wives, girlfriends or any person they had made love with prior to this trip that there could be a chance that they might be infected with whatever the sailor was suffering from, and to go get a checkup. The form was to be sent to anyone listed on it by the crewman. Well, these guys would come unglued and they would say, "I'll give you anything if you don't make me fill out that paper and I'll even pay you to treat me on the side." Of course I put on a little show explaining how much trouble I could be on the wrong end of by doing this. The more trouble I told them I could be in, the deeper they would dig into their pockets. These people were coming up with rolls of cash. I don't know where they got all that money but I do know they were very well paid for their jobs. And I *could* have gotten into serious difficulty. But I saved them a lot of embarrassment and perhaps even taught them a little lesson along the way. Isn't American ingenuity great?

We returned home with the troops and my discharge was awaiting me. I packed my bags, said goodbye to the U.S. Navy, walked through the gates of Treasure Island, gave them one last salute and became a civilian. So, now what?

Chapter Six

A SHORT CHAPTER FOR A SHORT MARRIAGE

After I returned home and settled down a bit, I started college to brush up on some prerequisites I needed to get into one of the major universities. While I was in school, I started going steady with a beautiful and sweet young lady whose parents were Yugoslavian. We dated for some time. Then one night I asked Dutch to be the best man at my wedding in Reno. He agreed to do that and did it well. Bingo, I was a married man.

Shortly after that, Dutch moved to Seattle, Washington and started going to barber college in Bremerton while I still had hopes of getting into a medical school and continuing my medical pursuits. The closer I got to my goal the more I could see that there was way on earth that I could do this because I simply didn't have the funds for it. I was heartbroken as I could see my life-long ambition disappearing before my eyes. I was in despair because I knew I had the gift of the physician and had the knowledge to pursue it along with a love for medicine and an even greater love for humanity. After talking with some of the medical students whom I met and who really didn't give a damn about medicine but were there only because their fathers and grandfathers were doctors and would pay their way through medical school, it just didn't seem fair to me. But I still gave it a shot and almost killed myself in the process. I was going to school, doing five hours of homework every night and working from two to six in the morning cooking hamburgers at a local hamburger place. I got off work with just enough time to go home, take a shower and return to school for class. I lost about 35 pounds in six months and eventually had to give it up. There was no way I could continue on that way. I bitterly decided that my medical career was to be a thing of the past and began to think of some way to make a living.

I still had some money left in my government college education fund from my stint in the Navy. This wasn't enough to finish medical school by a long shot but there was enough there for me to join Dutch up in Bremerton and attend barber college. It was a terribly difficult choice, but I had to do something and at least I'd be with my brother.

So my wife and I moved up to Seattle, Washington. Dutch and I would take the ferry across Puget Sound every day to the college. I found another opportunity in this hour-long ferry ride. There were quite a few passengers aboard the ferry that played pinochle every trip for pocket change. It wasn't anything like my vitamin C caper, but Dutch and I always made enough money to pay our round trip fares on the ferry. We were just better card players than most.

Both of us finished barber college and Dutch went back to California, took the state board test and passed it. I graduated soon after Dutch. My wife was getting homesick at the time and her parents lived in Bisbee, Arizona. Before I tied myself down to a steady job it seemed like a good time to take my wife back to her parents. Let's face it, we weren't getting along too well and we were having a lot of arguments. I understood that things had been rough on her but I had great hopes of our marriage improving now that I had my barber's license. We did go to Arizona but instead of getting better the situation worsened. After round after round of our seemingly eternal fight I told her I was tired of the tension and I wanted to leave and our separation was amicable.

Chapter Seven

HIGH SOCIETY ON THE HIGH SEAS

I found myself back in Concord checking around for all job opportunities. I didn't find anything exciting or appealing enough to pursue and felt that there had to be something better out there...somewhere.

I'd started a new social life and one night I had a dinner date with a girl in San Francisco. We followed dinner with cocktails in the restaurant's lounge. We didn't want to leave too early as it was always better to wait until the later hours to cross the Oakland Bay Bridge going home because the traffic thinned out by then and it was a pleasant drive after midnight.

Before leaving for home that night I became acquainted with a gentleman sitting at the bar and as we talked he asked what I did for a living. I told him I was a barber but "between jobs" at the time. I didn't know it, but a knew phase in my life was just around the corner. This man asked me if I would be interested in taking on the barbershop on board a luxury liner. It seemed that the man who had the barbershop

51

had suffered a heart attack and would be hospitalized for some time. I asked my new friend a lot of questions about the job and what it would take to start. He told me the first thing I would have to do was get cleared by the F.B I. and get what is known as a "Z" card which would give me the right to go ashore anyplace in the world. This sounded like an exciting thing to try. I was free now. I didn't have to worry about my wife or anything else. Maybe I could really have some fun on this ship. I told the man I would do it. In a very short time I found myself aboard a beautiful luxury liner being escorted by an uniformed porter to my stateroom where I would live during my travels. The stateroom was close to the barber and beauty shop and it was a very comfortable cabin, a heck of a lot better than what I had grown used to in the Navy. I began thinking I had fallen into something really beautiful here!

Next day we steamed out of San Francisco and I made a walking tour of the ship. It was a most wonderful vessel in all ways. The beautiful dining room had a golden staircase, with crystal chandeliers everywhere. I was very pleased with myself for finding this most unusual and terrific position.

The ship's itinerary included Honolulu, Manila, Japan, Yokosuka, Kobe, Hong Kong and Singapore, then back to Japan, Honolulu and San Francisco. It was a two-month trip to some of the best ports in the world. I was looking forward to a super voyage and was not disappointed once. Right away I began to get to know some very interesting people. Barbering has its advantages!

The passengers were in a much more rarified class of people than I was used to. They had a great deal of money. They had to be quite well off to afford the trip they were taking. There were doctors, judges and professionals of all sorts. Most of them were elegant people who took the good things in life in stride. I couldn't help but be impressed. This was a very different thing for me, being around such opulence. It seemed to me that these wealthy folks belonged to a class all their own. Everyone I met was kind to me and I tried to return each kindness.

On this voyage I met Dr. Norman Vincent Peale. He and his family were combining a vacation with some work he was doing out in the Philippine Islands. I was lucky and got to spend some time with him just talking and getting to know him. He was one of the most interesting passengers I met. He took the time to talk with me. Everything he said too made such sense. I have his words locked in memory to this day. He was a wonderful man. He was a doctor of metaphysics and his beliefs were very simple: what you say and do will come back to you. He believed that our lives should be led very positively and negativity had to be cast aside. I don't claim to have understood all the things he tried to explain, but I admired his patience as he tried to enlighten me.

Even though I had spent what felt like a lifetime on ships at sea, I found I hadn't found my sea legs for my new job. There was a world of difference between running around selling spiked oranges, and cutting hair with a pair of sharp scissors and a razor. I needed a different sort of "sea legs". I'd noticed a little strap with a buckle on the barber chair and didn't know what it was for . . . until we hit rough weather. I found I could hook myself up to it, lean back and just move with the motion of the ship.

As night fell on my first day at sea on my new ship I did what I always did to get used to any new vessel. Walking as far as I could to the forward part of the ship I did a little bow riding. Try it sometime if you have the opportunity. Go as far forward as possible and as the bow comes out of the water you will feel the tremendous power of the sea and the next thing you'll be dropping down with a light sense of weightlessness. The spray of the ocean will caress your face and before you know it you'll have your sea legs and you'll find yourself walking *with* the ship instead of against it.

Aside from the additional comfort aboard this civilian-operated liner, I discovered other differences. Familiar objects had different names than what I was used to in the service. Bulkheads became walls. The ladder became the staircase. In the Navy we were under the command of the Captain, but here he was called the Commodore. The Commodore's second in command was the First Mate, not the Executive Officer I was used to. While having no problems adjusting to the rather pampered life aboard the luxury liner, *President Cleveland*, I did have a few things to learn.

That first cruise was beautifully smooth for the most part, and time seemed to just melt away. I was always busy, seven days a week. After breakfast I would go to work, take a short break in the afternoon and after work I'd schmooze with the passengers and have a few drinks. After work I could do just about anything I wanted to. I took care of my business, though. There were over eight hundred passengers on board and they depended on me for all their hair needs, as they didn't want to get haircuts ashore because they didn't know the barbers, the sanitary conditions or even the language spoken in our ports-of-call.

It took five days to sail from San Francisco to Honolulu. I'd been there so many times it was practically like a second hometown to me. Sailing into Pearl Harbor is a majestic sight. The first thing you see on the approach to Honolulu is the magnificent Diamond Head volcano at one end of Waikiki Beach and then pretty soon you find yourself steaming into the harbor. I had plenty of shore liberty on this ship. After we docked I was usually the first one down the gangplank . . . and the last one back! Mostly I just partied and met people. The ship was just like a magical moveable hotel. I couldn't dream of any hotel in Honolulu that could be better than my cabin on the *President Cleveland*.

By the time we left Hawaii I was starting to get to know some of the other crewmen, the First and Second Mates and Commodore Eman. The Commodore was a fine man. He was an elderly, soft-spoken, brilliant sea captain who had spent his whole life on the water. He was an elegant human being and he knew how to handle people. He loved his ship, passengers and crew and he certainly loved his job. It seems to me that those things make up the ingredients for a happy and fulfilling life. I always enjoyed talking with him and he always seemed to have plenty of time to reciprocate. One thing that always surprised me about Commodore Eman was that he was always checking to see if I was comfortable and that I had everything I needed. I felt that my captain actually respected his barber. It meant a lot. He probably didn't realize that I was thrilled just to be there and hadn't even expected the accommodations I had been given.

Every time we left port there was a twenty-piece band playing as the ship pulled away from the dock. All the passengers would throw confetti and streamers off the decks and it was always a gala event. The bands always played the same song, *Around the World in 80 Days*.

After leaving Honolulu we sailed south to do the Philippine Islands. This part of the world is in the Southern Hemisphere and as we arrived at night it was absolutely breathtaking. The sky was so dark and the stars so close, it felt like a person could snatch a star right out of the heavens and take it home for a souvenir. When the moon rises here, it is so large that it is hard to describe what it looks like, sort of like a great white ball that just pops out of the ocean and rises above you slowly and surely until it becomes a bright orb in the dark sky. I used to love to go to the highest point on the highest deck and lay on my back and watch the stars and the moon. This is such a humbling event, with the large and expansive dark sky dotted with prisms of light from horizon to horizon. What wonders God provides for His children! I sometimes wonder today if I'll ever get the chance to do this again some day. That would be such a treat.

Pulling into Manila we went through the same routine as in Hawaii. Some of our guests would disembark and others would join us. I said goodbye to Dr. Peale and his family at this port, telling him how much I enjoyed meeting all of them and how much I treasured our talks. He gave me his card and said that he would be home in a couple of months and that I should give him a call. I wish now that I had, but I never did. Now he's gone and it's too late.

We spent three or four days in Manila allowing plenty of time for the passengers to see the sights and buy their souvenirs. These islands are beautiful and some people call them "The Pearls of the Pacific." I was able to see how beautiful they really were, as our ship passed quite near several of them. I remember they were plush green with lots of palm trees and waterfalls.

At sea, between ports I had a great time. Fortunately I love the sea. I would go to sea right now if the right opportunity arose. Some folks can't take the ocean but I absolutely love it. When it's my time to die I hope my ashes will be strewn as far out to sea as possible.

Out of Manila Bay our ship was pointed toward Yokohama, Japan. The passengers were really excited about going there. Remember that this was in the nineteen-fifties and it was only about ten years after World War II. Many of the cities weren't rebuilt yet after the huge amount of damage caused by the war. Tokyo, Yokosuka and Yokohama were well on their way toward complete reconstruction, however. These cities were fairly close together and very large. Each one had large open-air markets where we could buy whatever our hearts wanted. You could get beautiful natural pearls for a song. Ornate China settings were most reasonable and cost hundreds of dollars less than back home.

Kobe was another delightful and beautiful city. We happened to arrive when the cherry blossoms were in bloom. There were thousands of trees blossoming all over the place and the sight was inspiring.

Please remember that at this time Japan had not been totally Westernized and they still had their old Japanese customs and traditions. As you walked down a street you might see a man striding about ten paces ahead of his wife, both dressed in kimonos with *hobes* on their backs.

They would be wearing little wooden shoes and the woman would have her hair up in a huge bun combed with wax to keep its shape. Long wooden needles would secure the bun. I thought they were beautiful people with beautiful customs, and also a very honest people. The Japanese might also be the cleanest race in history. Bathing is such a ritual that I don't have the room to go into it in these pages. Nobody walks into a Japanese home with shoes on, either. You must remove them at the door and proceed from there in your socks. This isn't just for cleanliness . . . they have rice mats covering the spotless floors, and shoes (especially wooden shoes) would wear them out.

As we left Kobe there was the usual bon voyage with the local musicians giving us a reprise of *Around the World*. You might think it would be boring after awhile, hearing the same song, but life aboard this great ship was never boring! The atmosphere was charged with excitement and happiness for the new passengers coming aboard at each new port. This mood was infectious. It always seemed to me that I was privileged to be invited to a grand party and I could hardly wait to see who else was invited. I always knew I was going to meet a bunch of fun, terrific new people and I'll tell you it was a blast!

Our next stop was Hong Kong. There was no duty in Hong Kong and there was such a melange of all nationalities here, it breathed excitement. This was *the* place to shop. Custom tailored suits for $35US or a handmade sport coat for $30US. The passengers were indulging in a shopping frenzy, purchasing custom made clothing, pearls, jade, sapphires, diamonds, watches and just about everything else under the sun. Rugs, statuary, linens . . . the list goes on and on. There was nothing you couldn't get in Hong Kong.

Across from Hong Kong there was a large business center. At that time England controlled Hong Kong and the Brits did a lot of business in this port. A short ferry ride from Hong Kong got you to Macao, which was a Portuguese settlement and was also known as the Las Vegas of the Orient. There was a big gambling zone and it was a wild place to be. It was a little spooky because it was kind of like going back in time to the days when you had to watch your back and be careful of shadowy places because there might be some thug lurking to steal your winnings and maybe even take your life.

Three days in Hong Kong and off to Singapore. I think that Singapore is the cleanest city I have ever seen. It looks like the people wash the streets every day. You never see anything on the ground. There is a large fine for discarding a candy wrapper or even crushing out a cigarette out on the ground. However, there are refuse containers all over the place so there is really no reason to litter. There was also Raffles Hotel, which was where the famous Singapore Sling was invented. The first time I went there, I asked about the their famous cocktail and the bartender said that yes, it was created there and that if I could drink two of them I would receive the rest of my drinks free for the rest of the evening. I thought that was a great deal, as I was a pretty darned good drinker in those days. Well, I don't remember making it to the third one! I *do* remember that the room had developed a spinning motion and I had to go outside to breathe some fresh air.

After our three days in Singapore we sailed back through Yokohama and the other ports until we returned and found ourselves back in San Francisco. I was looking forward to the next trip, which would normally have started within five days of our arrival. But a few days before we got home a telegram reached the ship that told us the liner was going into dry dock for fifty-two days.

I, along with the rest of the crew, took all of our personal stuff after we docked. We were to report back just before the fifty-two days were up. "Have a nice vacation," said the company executives. The previous night, the last of the trip, I was playing poker down on C deck with some of the crew. I was lucky and won quite a bit of money. After all, fifty-two days without a paycheck is a long time.

After we docked the whole crew was scrambling to get off the ship. I walked away feeling sad about leaving. There were many memories there and some of the things that happened changed my life permanently. For one thing, I had become used to this elegant new way of life and the rich people who inhabited it. They were, to me, "perfect people." They were so well spoken and intelligent. I hoped that a little had rubbed off on me. You weren't going to see me in just any cheap bar from now on, not me. The Mark Hopkins Hotel, at the Top of the Mark, is the ritziest watering hole in the city and was just waiting for my business. There I would find the same kind of people I'd gotten used to on the ship, that class of people with refined tastes and big bucks. Let's face it. I was a budding social climber. I couldn't help it. I really liked being around those folks. During this period in life I was saying to myself, "Where there's a will there's a way and one of these days I'm going to be right up there, living in style. I'm young and intelligent and I'll find some way to do it."

I was standing on the dock thinking about all this, gazing at the *President Cleveland* with a pocket full of poker winnings and fifty-two days on my hands when I heard a familiar and loved voice calling my name. It was my sister Althea and my brother Dutch was with her. They had driven over from Concord to pick me up and before we left I gave them a tour of the ship so they could see for themselves how gorgeous it was.

As we drove back to Concord, Dutch said he had a surprise for me. The surprise turned out to be a job in the best shop in town. But somehow I didn't feel like going to work. I just couldn't see myself growing old, being an old barber in some neighborhood . . . just growing older and older and nothing happening. I'd tasted a little bit of the good life and I just knew there was something better than the rat race. It was out there, and it was waiting for me. I was going to find it if it killed me. I was absolutely determined, but I didn't know just what it was I was searching for.

I had to tell Dutch that I needed time to think about things and he understood because he and I have always been on the same wavelength. He wanted to know what I was planning on doing and I told him that I was going to get a good night sleep and in the morning I was going to toss a coin. "That's right, Dutch. I'm going to take a quarter out of my pocket and flip it. If the coin comes up Heads, I'm going to take my car and head south. I don't know how far I'm going, but I'm going. Tails and I'm driving north. If the darn quarter stands on its edge I'll go east because I just came from the west."

Next morning I found myself on the road as promised, and the morning sun was to my left. That quarter had come up Heads and it turned out to be a beautiful drive down to Los Angeles. The wildflowers were in bloom and the weather was an absolutely ideal.

Chapter Eight

FINDING MYSELF IN PARADISE

After an all day drive it was close to sunset and I was tired and hungry. I had driven straight through L.A., still heading south and I started looking for a place to pull over and saw a sign that read "NEWPORT BEACH...HARBOR BLVD." I followed the big arrow off the freeway, thinking to myself that this might be just the place I wanted to be. I passed a little town called Costa Mesa and finally found myself in a jewel of a spot called Newport Harbor which included Newport Beach, Balboa, Corona del Mar and several islands, each with a somewhat nautical name. There was Harbor Island, Shark Island, Balboa Island, Newport Island, Lido Island and a couple of others.

First off, I found a nice restaurant sitting right on the bay. I figured it must be a good one because the parking lot was full. Since I was alone I walked up to the bar and ordered a drink, noticing some guys in the back tossing darts. The loser had to buy the next round of drinks. This looked like a lot of fun but a big steak and lobster dinner sounded even better. When I had finished eating and returned to the bar area the guys were still at their dart game and I asked one of them if he knew of a good hotel. He said there were "thousands" of places to stay. He asked who I was and I told him and he introduced himself and the other players, and the next thing you know I'm in there throwing darts, too. These guys were the friendliest people I'd ever met. They didn't know me from Adam, but they treated me like I was a lifelong buddy.

Lo and behold, one of these guys was a barber. His name was René Mortelette and we became friends instantly. He mentioned that he had a shop in the Lido Island shopping area and he was going out of town to Pittsburgh to see the Pirates play baseball. He asked me if I could run his shop while he was gone. I must have an honest face. I mean I just met this guy! Well, I told him that I was back from two months at sea on the *President Cleveland* and this fascinated him. I explained that the ship was in dry dock and that I could hardly wait until she sailed again because the next trip was going around the world. I gave him a short synopsis of my first cruise and he was hanging on every word. René and I became pretty close pals in a very short time. He made me promise to at least stop by his shop before I left town so he could show it off to me and I told him I sure would.

There I was, bright and early next morning in front of René's store, which was really in a sweet location right in the middle of all the Lido Island activity. I had learned that Lido Island is quite an exclusive place. If you live there you're into big money. Today, just a 30-foot lot would go for well over $1,000,000 and that's just the *lot* with no house.

The more I hung around Newport the more I liked it. It was high summer and everything about the place was fascinating to me. Everyone was running around barefoot all over the place and they were just casual, beautiful people. I had plenty of time before my ship sailed so I decided to spend at least another week there. This would give René a chance to head for Pittsburgh for his baseball game. I agreed to watch his shop for him and told him to take off. Just like that he handed me the key to his store and walked out the door with a big smile.

The next morning I got up extra early and showered and shaved. I was ready to start the day at Lido's Shaving Mug Barbershop on Lido Island. I didn't know what to expect, but all of René's tools were there and I was ready to go. The shop opened at 9am so I went in at eight-thirty to put the change in the register and let the other two barbers and the manicurist in. I introduced myself to them and explained that I would be running the place while René was in Pittsburgh and I assured them that we would all be working together as friends "And now let's open up and get the day started," urged the temporary new boss.

After we opened for business I got the shock of my life. The very first two customers who walked through the door were giants. I mean they were *big* people. As they came in the sun was blocked out! When I looked up, I saw whom it was I couldn't believe my eyes. There stood my film idol, John Wayne. With the Duke was another actor, Victor McLaglen. Duke sat down in my chair and this was the beginning of a great friendship. I came to absolutely love Duke. He was a down to earth guy. He just wanted a little trim and expressed that he didn't have much hair and wanted to preserve what he had left. We both started laughing about it. I trimmed his hair just the way he wanted it and then asked him, "Do you come by the shop every week?" He said, "I can, if necessary." I said that I'd love to see him every week. From that day on he did come in for a "trim" and a chat every week if he was in town. You wouldn't believe the customers I had that first day. It seemed that every Hollywood star who lived on Lido Island needed their hair cut and they were all coming in to René's place to have it done. Not only did I trim Wayne and McLaglen this first day but also Ray Milland, Dana Andrews, Errol Flynn, Humphrey Bogart and Jimmy Cagney. Some of the most famous actors in the world turned out to be René's regulars. "I need a haircut and a manicure, please." "Oh, sure, Mr. Bogart." Whew! These people turned out to be just as friendly and normal as the proverbial guy next door. I got along well with them after I realized they were just "folks" no matter how talented they were. One day I was cutting Ray Milland's hair and I told him about my voyage on the *President Cleveland*. Even though Ray was a multi-millionaire he was a penny-pincher and he thought it was fantastic that a fellow like me could get on that ship and work myself around the world without laying out a dime. He was writing for a magazine at the time and he was so interested in the ship and my story that he wrote five pages right then and there about his barber whom got paid to travel on luxury liners!

While I was doing my stand-in for René at the barbershop I was surprised to find that there was quite a few customers who came back the very next day after getting their haircuts just to shoot the breeze. I was starting to make a lot of friends during these "bull sessions". One of these guys was the captain of a 105-foot yacht who went by the name "Cappie". A lot of the rich owners of these dream yachts didn't know how to run their own boats and would hire full-time crews to sail them and maintain them.

Cappie wasn't the only one with a nautical nickname. It seemed that everyone down there had something to do with boating. One of my fondest dreams for years was to own my very own boat, maybe a 40 or 50-footer, motor sailor, ketch rig, twin diesel engines. In my mind I knew exactly what I wanted and I would find myself piloting this fantasy in my dreams.

René's shop was located in a building that also had a restaurant called The Blue Dolphin. This was a very popular place for lunch, which was very good for the barbershop. In order to get into the restaurant everyone had to walk right by our place. It seemed that every time I looked up I'd recognize someone from the movie industry like Jane Powell or Eleanor Parker, Claire Trevor, Milton Bren and on and on.

Rock Hudson, a friendly and interesting guy had moved to Lido Island and everyone was breaking his or her neck to make him comfortable. He was a shooting star and everyone knew it. I was a bit lost because I had lost contact with the latest movies while I was working at sea. I had a little catching up to do.

After all, it was embarrassing to have a big movie star ask me what I thought such and such picture he was in and I hadn't even seen it. I began spending a lot of time at movie theaters. In that week I discovered that there was absolutely no class distinction in Newport Beach. It was nothing to see a movie star walking down the road with a house painter or carpenter. If someone was interesting it didn't matter what kind of work they did.

The main reason why so many celebrities and others with great means or fame live in Newport Beach is this: It's called "fun". The area has seven islands, and yachts surround every one of them. These people live in Newport to be near their boats so they can take their weekend jaunts to Mexico or Santa Barbara or Catalina Island, which is about 24 miles off the coast. The miles of pristine beaches (in those days) held a certain attraction, too. A lot of the residents practically spent their lives on the beach. It was the home of big time tanning. A typical N.B. day might go like this. Come home from work. Put on bathing suit. Go to beach and swim and body surf. Meet friends at beach, build big bonfire, play volleyball. Have big cookout on beach and after dinner break out the guitars and ukes and sing to the moon and stars. Maybe later on it would be fun to hop into someone's boat and cruise the canals, still singing, and maybe stop at a few bistros that sported docks. Okay, maybe that wasn't *typical* but it was the ideal, especially on weekends.

There was no shortage of great restaurants in Newport Beach along with a number of cocktail lounges. Some that I remember from the time are still there. Some of these places were very classy and others were "local" bars where ordinary people like boat workers would mingle with the super-rich. Everyone was having a great time. There was also the huge Rendezvous Ballroom, which was built way back in the twenties. What a terrific place that was. During the Big Band Era, every great orchestra and every top vocalist played there. Under the four-story-high ceiling, there was a raised bandstand and a huge dance floor. Surrounding the dance floor was a second floor balcony with places to sit and enjoy your drinks and snacks. The Rendezvous was located in Balboa, where you could also find the Fun Zone, with its penny arcades and a little Ferris wheel and carousel.

The ballroom was still going strong when I first arrived in Newport Beach and you could still dance your tail off there. It was a kinder, gentler time compared to what we have today.

For a few bucks you could have the most fun imaginable. But time marches on and as the years went by the old ballroom's popularity waned. But the dark and empty old landmark didn't just fade away with a whimper. The Rendezvous Ballroom went out with a bang. It burned down one night in a spectacular blaze. But what a sad loss for those of us who can recall so many fun times spent there.

Newport Beach is ideally located. It is fifty miles south of Beverly Hills and the Hollywood area, just far enough for the L.A. crowd to feel they are "getting away for the weekend" but close enough to get back on Sunday and be ready for work Monday morning. In the fifties it was a real paradise.

Unfortunately, today Newport Beach has become Los Angeles by the sea. There are so many boats docked there now that you can barely see the water. Instead of the old sleepy winters of the fifties when the tourists all went home, people live there all year 'round. Traffic is a nightmare. The beautiful old coves are crammed with houses. Progress? It's really a shame but I feel I had the best of it and had it that way for years and years. Was I lucky, or what?

Most of the names of the actor's boats were synonymous with their personalities. Duke

Wayne's boat was *The Wild Goose* and she was gorgeous. One hundred and forty feet long, she was a converted icebreaker that he brought down from Alaska and converted into a luxury yacht. This was some refurbishing job! I saw the ship when he first brought her down before the conversion and was knocked out with what he did do her. The first thing Duke did was raised all of the doorways. The Duke was a tall son-of-a-gun and didn't especially enjoy banging his head. He put in chandeliers and all sorts of wonderful amenities. He loved that boat with a passion. He used her a great deal and made some great voyages on her. He especially liked to take her down to Mexico. If you saw the "Wild Goose" flag flying it meant that Duke was aboard.

The Lady Claire belonged to Claire Trevor. Her husband, Milton Bren who was another very nice guy, built it for her. Milt and I became friends and he really helped me out a lot in Newport Beach and he deserves my deepest thanks.

Another fine yacht, a 60-foot schooner, was known as the *Santana*. She was owned at various times by several top stars. Everyone loved her and everyone wanted her. The first owner I remember was Humphrey Bogart and he spent a lot of time aboard her. I believe the next owner was Dick Powell and I think he sold it to Ray Milland.

James Cagney owned *The Red Witch* and Rock Hudson's yacht was called *Sheherezade*. Errol Flynn had a boat named *Cirraco*, a sleek, black hulled schooner rig. Joe LaShelle had an interesting craft that looked like a PT boat called *Vagrant*. Joe was a famous cinematographer who won several Academy Awards for his work. One of his famous movies was *Marty* with Ernest Borgnine. Jim Arness had the *Seasmoke*, named after his TV show, *Gunsmoke*, and Bell Tye's boat was named *Rinnee II*.

Not all the stars had yachts, but the majority of them did. There were times when one of my famous friends would invite me along for a cruise to Avalon, the only town on Catalina Island. It would amaze me to find myself, an unknown, being on a first name basis and treated as an equal by these people. Where else in the world would this have been possible? Easy familiarity aside, I will never lose my great respect for these people who worked hard for the position they held. If you are a movie star, you have earned it.

Chapter Nine

THE YANKEE CLIPPER

Well, as you might have guessed, I never went back to the *President Cleveland*. I wasn't about to leave my newfound paradise. Instead, I worked for René for a couple of years and I built up a great clientele. By this time I wanted my own business, more of a salon for men's styling instead of just a barbershop. I began to scout around for a location. One area around Lido Island had a great appeal to me and I'd go there two or three times a week and just sit there picturing what I could do with it. This location was right on the bay where you could look out the window and see the walkway along the water, and it had a great view of all the beautiful yachts in the bay. This was a premium location and was bound to come with a premium price.

I tried working with a property manager but he and I didn't get along so well. Every time I asked him about my chosen spot and what it would cost to rent it he would always be vague and say things like, "If you have to ask, you can't afford it." This kind of talk really put a damper on my plans so I kind of put it out of my mind. But one day I was talking to Milton Bren about this property manager and how he had treated me and Milt told me that guy had a lot to learn about business. Milt then asked me if I knew who owned the property. I said that I didn't, and Milt told me the property belonged to Dick Powell. It turned out that Mr. Powell owned many properties in Newport and Milt began pointing out all the buildings and docks in the Powell collection. Milt advised me to meet with Dick and discuss the property personally. Milton wouldn't give me Dick's phone number but he did tell me where the Powell residence was and suggested that I write a short letter explaining what I wanted to do and then drive by the house and leave the letter in his mailbox. I asked Milton if Dick would even read it. He told me that Dick would either both tear it up and toss it and throw it away or more likely he would give me a call. Milt told me Dick was a great guy and he turned out to be right. In fact, Dick Powell turned out to be one of the best friends I've ever had.

He was a giant in the movie and television industry and a great businessman, too. He had taken time from his movie acting career to form a corporation called Four Star Television Productions. Dick's partners in this venture were Ida Lupino, Charles Boyer and David

Niven. I believe that later on Robert Taylor was brought into the company. It took a genius to put it together and keep it going. Dick was the president and he deserves all the credit. Some of the stars of the many TV programs he created were Steve McQueen, Nick Adams, Telly Savalas, Robert Faulk, Gene Barry and others.

So I wrote my letter and drove by and deposited it in the Powell mailbox. I expected that if he could help, he would have someone call me or perhaps he'd drop me a line. Two days later who should walk into René's for a haircut? You guessed it, Dick Powell. I began to cut his hair, reeling off a couple of good jokes (what's a barber for?) and he tells me a few and we're having a great time. It was close to noon when I finished with the cut and Dick asked me if I'd eaten lunch yet and I said no but I sure was hungry. He said, "Come on. I'll buy you lunch at the Dolphin." While we were eating, he asked me what I wanted to put in his building. I explained what a man's styling shop was and he gave me a hard time about turning into a beautician and we both had a good laugh about that. He wanted to know if I would still be able to give him a plain old haircut and I said that he could have anything he wanted. He wanted to know why I felt a styling shop would go over in a little place like Newport. I told him that I just knew it and that if I was wrong I could still do plain old barbering. He asked me how many chairs I was planning on and I told him I'd start out with three. Then I told him about the other things that I wanted to add. "Are these *other things* legal?" he asked and we both laughed. We talked over my plans for a long time and I drew out on a napkin what I wanted the shop to look like. But, I explained to him, I didn't know if I had enough money to start this thing up. I let him know that I wasn't a rich man but that I was a hard worker and I was clean and friendly and that was the best thing I could offer him. He studied the layout and I told him about the panoramic view from the chairs looking at the yachts. He liked that a lot because the first boat you would see was his own yacht, *Sapphire Sea*. In fact he was bringing her in that evening. She was a beauty at 105 feet and she was spotless.

Dick liked everything he heard. Finally, after I had told him where I wanted everything in the shop to go including the shoeshine stand, I got to where I wanted to put the bar. His eyebrows shot up. "You're going to sell booze?" "No, no," I laughed, "I'm going to *give* it away." Naturally, he wanted to know how in the world anyone could run a business by giving away free drinks. I explained that my business plan called for the manicurist to double as bartender.

"That's fine, but I still don't understand the free drinks. Where's the profit and the end of the day?" "Well," I replied, "You've asked a lot of questions today except the most important one . . . what's the price of the haircut? It's really a pretty simple thing, Dick. If you want a martini I'll *give* you one but I'll also add a couple of bucks to the price of your haircut. I'm not selling *drinks*, just haircuts. If I started selling alcohol the State Board of Examiners and Alcoholic Beverage Control would close me down in a minute. But I do have the right to give a drink to anyone as a customer.

Dick stared at me for a second and then roared with laughter and suggested that we take a walk down to my proposed location and look around. We took a quick stroll down to the building and went into the office. My nemesis, the property manager was there and Dick turned to this guy and said, "Now listen to me very carefully. This is Glenn Maxwell and he is a very good friend of mine. You give him that location and let him pay whatever he wants to pay and help him as much as you can to getting him established." I couldn't believe I was hearing this. I almost fell over. Turning to me he said, "Glenn, I want you to start off real easy because the equipment you want to buy is going to be expensive and it's easy to over-extend yourself." I could only thank him as profusely as possible while we walked back to his car. He told me to get started any time I wanted and he would have the property manager get me a key that day. He drove off leaving me standing there on the sidewalk in total awe—and elation.

It was at this time that my estranged wife made an appearance. She popped into Newport Beach one day and we had lunch together. We agreed that each of us could do better without the other and during that one luncheon we arranged for a divorce. We wished each other luck and happiness then went off on our separate ways and have always maintained our friendship. If you are thinking that so far I have been the luckiest guy in history, you might be right.

For the next few months my daily routine was to get off work and go over to Berkshire's, which was my favorite hangout and happened to be located right next to my new "salon". I'd have a couple of drinks and then go next door and work on my store. I worked hard and long getting the place ready to open as fast as possible. Every night I'd have carpenters and plumbers there doing the extensive remodeling the shop needed to get what I wanted out of it. It was beginning to look the way I had seen it in my mind's eye and I was one excited barber.

On one of those evenings that I was working, I took a break and was sitting out enjoying the beautiful sunset across the bay. I was sitting on a bench just relaxing and smoking a cigarette, when Rock Hudson came strolling by. We struck up a conversation and he inquired about how things were going with the shop (nothing went on around there that everyone didn't know about.) He asked me what I was going to name it. I said I hadn't come up with anything as yet but I knew that I'd better get around to it pretty quick because I was almost ready to open. He suggested that The Yankee Clipper might be appropriate for the harbor area. That sounded just fine to me and I told him he had just named my new business and thanked him.

I didn't see him until about two weeks after that. When I did see him next, he gave me a beautiful portfolio with blank checks, a record book, and an endorsement stamp for checks, all of them with a painstakingly detailed schooner design imprinted on them. It was his open house gift to me and I just couldn't thank him enough. The printing was exquisite. This was about the time he was finalizing the purchase of his new yacht and he invited me down to see her. We did, and I found she was even more beautiful close in than she was from afar. I asked Rock if he knew how to sail her and he said he didn't but he was looking forward to learning how. I said that if I could get some time off from work I would take him out and teach him what he needed to know. Everyone liked Rock Hudson and I was no exception.

I had been working so hard at René's shop during the day and in my own shop at night that I decided when the weekend came, I was going to just relax. It was Friday morning and a bunch of buddies of mine came into René's all excited about a big party happening Saturday night at Christian's Hut. This was a Polynesian-style dinner house and saloon, very dark on the inside and was a good place to eat. The name was derived from the book *Mutiny on the Bounty* and it's famous character, Mr. Christian. It was right on the bay and there was a big outrigger on its side on the beach out in front. Huge palm trees surrounded the building, which had a grass roof, and a person could really get into the illusion of being transported to some tropical island. The bar was a little primitive, but that was the idea and this was a great place to party. So you got loaded and spilled your drink. Who cared? I don't remember the reason for the Saturday party but I do remember that just about everyone I knew showed up for it.

After work on Saturday, I headed over to the party with one of my pals. It was already going strong and a lot people were already a bit tanked, some completely blitzed and they were all singing and dancing. Now, I was tired from working all day and I hadn't eaten lunch, either. I started in on Mai Tai's and after a few, I was definitely feeling the rum. We were all having a ball but as it got later and later I began running out of steam. I walked outside to get some much-needed fresh air and the last thing I remember is laying under a palm tree on the beach. To make it brief, I passed out.

I woke up the next morning with a hot sun blasting down on me and I didn't have a clue where I was. I had a stomach ache, my tongue tasted like a zookeeper's heel and I felt dirty and needed a shower. The pounding headache wasn't that wonderful, either. Some kind soul had come along in the night and covered me with newspaper. I felt pathetic. I was struggling to figure out where I was and what time it was and getting my eyes adjusted to the bright light of day. I figured it was still early, as the sun was low in the sky. Then I gingerly sat up and found I wasn't alone. Lying right next to me was another body. I coughed to clear my throat, waking up the poor guy in the process. He, too, was covered with newspapers (maybe he was the one who had covered me) and as he slid yesterday's headlines from his face there appeared the unmistakable visage of Lee Marvin. He peered my way and said in that rumbling voice of his, "Where can I get a drink?" Wow! I told him the only place I could think of was Berkshire's, but that it was quite away down the road. I knew we wouldn't have any trouble getting in even if the place was closed because I knew the janitor. Lee thought this was a fine idea. Neither of us had a car so we started off to walk the mile or so to shelter and blessed relief. A few minutes after we set off, we came across a little old lady just getting into her car on her way to church and I asked her if she happened to be headed towards Lido Island. Then Lee staggered up and she recognized him. Ah, the perks of fame. She was happy to give us a lift right to the door of Berkshire's. The bar was just opening up and the party started all over again. Lee and I spent the whole day bar hopping and I think we hit 'em all.

It was about two days before the proud Grand Opening of The Yankee Clipper. I was working with René and despite my joy at having my own business opening in a few days, I was feeling a little sad about leaving René and the rest of the staff. These people had been my pals for more than two years. Well, we were still close enough to play Gin Rummy and bet on all the football and basketball games. Anyway, I got a call in the late afternoon from Rock Hudson. He wanted to know if I could knock off from work a little early and meet him down at The Yankee Clipper because he had a little surprise for me. I told him I'd be right there.

Whatever you might have heard or read about Rock Hudson I can tell you he was unbelievably thoughtful and generous. I went down to the Clipper and opened it up. Rock was already there and had some workmen dismantling the big picture window overlooking the bay and all the yachts. I asked what the heck he was doing and he said he was replacing the window with something I'd just love. I wanted to know what it was because I already loved my picture window and its view. The window was one of the main reasons I'd wanted the shop there in the first place. Grinning, Rock led me out to a big truck in the parking lot. The truck belonged to a glass company and unveiled my surprise. He showed me this huge double paned glass sheet that was hand etched with a four-masted sailing schooner which matched the embossed ship he had made up for my checks. Those workers placed that etched window where the plain glass window had been and when the lights were dimmed it looked magnificent and didn't take a thing away from the view, but rather added to it. This was one heck of an expensive gift. And that's the way Rock was. What a wonderful surprise and it just made the shop. Thanks again Rock, for being an Earth Angel to me.

On the opening day of my shop I made sure to get down there really early to make sure that all was perfect. Walking over from the parking lot I was stunned to see at least fifty people standing around just waiting my arrival for the opening! Flowers and plants were delivered and people came by with more flowers wishing me well on my Big Day. Rock Hudson and Dick Powell were both there along with so many other important and wonderful friends that, although I don't want to leave anyone out, I was so busy that day that I just can't remember right now who else was there. The sweet friendship of these people was overwhelming and it was a glorious time for me. In fact, I couldn't conceive that it could get any more glorious . . . until I looked out into the parking lot and saw a huge Channel 5 TV news truck that had come down all the way from Los Angeles to cover the opening of my little barbershop. To this day I have no idea who set this up (Dick Powell?), but the idea was ingenious. It was 8:50 am, ten minutes before my official opening. I had an inspiration and announced to the crowd that the first haircut in The Yankee Clipper would be on the house. To my great pleasure, the first customer in the chair was my cherished friend, Dick Powell. Champagne was flowing freely and people were milling around in and outside the shop.

Here is the scene. Dick is sitting in my chair and the Channel 5 lady is interviewing him and he is saying all these wonderful things about me. After she finishes with Dick, she interviews and tapes just about everyone in the place. I'm practically reeling with happiness. This program reaches millions and I'm getting all this publicity for absolutely nothing. What an advertising coup! Because of that one news feature I was eventually able to open up two more "salons" in exclusive areas in the region and they all became famous in Orange County where Newport Beach is located.

Needless to say, the Grand Opening was a great success. It was actually a little maddening to me with all these people coming in and out. Even after I'd finished doing their hair, people were not leaving. Everyone was hanging around and talking to each other and having drinks.

Around four in the afternoon a somewhat grubby guy came in. I was booked solid until

way past six. This guy was wearing deck shoes
without socks and an old pair of denims with a
hole in the knee and an old T-shirt that was
covered with paint. I figured him for one of the
deck hands on some yacht and I asked him if he
had an appointment. He said he didn't know
that he needed one. I told him that I really
needed space in the waiting area for those
patrons with appointments. I didn't want to be
rude to him especially since everyone in the
shop seemed to be watching our exchange.
Finally, I told him that if I had a cancellation I
would fit him in. "Meanwhile," I said, "I'll have
the manicurist fix you up with a drink and you
can sit outside." I'd set up a table with a big
umbrella and some chairs in front of the shop.
It was shady and cool and he could watch the
boats come in and out and await the hoped-for
cancellation. He didn't say a word to me. He
picked up a bourbon and water from the
manicurist and sat outside at the shaded table. I
was so busy that I forgot all about him. After
awhile some guys came in and said, "Glenn, do
you know who that is?" I told them I had no
idea but that I really did need room in the shop.
These guys started laughing so hard I thought
they'd die. "That's Howard Hughes!" someone
chortled. "You're the first person ever to throw
Howard Hughes out of a barber shop." I wish I

could tell you what a wonderful person Mr. Hughes was but I wouldn't know. I never got to know him as he disappeared before I could cut his hair. Sorry Howard, I would have enjoyed getting acquainted with you.

The rest of that day and the next three weeks were all alike . . . an absolute madhouse. I had so much business I could barely keep up. Finally things started smoothing out to a nice pace and once in awhile I could even take an hour off and have a cocktail at Berkshire's. My staff had the shop well in hand and I was in Berkshire's one day when Gary Cooper walked in with Ernest Hemingway. They were coming in for a cool one after relaxing on the beach. I had met Cooper before, but never Papa Hemingway. I said hi to Gary as they walked by me and was invited to their table. Hemingway had just finished writing *The Old Man and the Sea*. During the hour or so that I spent at the table I mentioned that I would love to write a book some day but had never studied writing. Papa asked me if I could tell a story and I said that I was good at that. He said, "Just tell the story and somebody will take care of the rest for you." I never forgot that advice and I've been keeping it mind as I work on this project. If you happen to be reading my book, I guess it was a very good tip!

The winter months were approaching and it was the end of October. Newport was getting back to normal. During the summer the tourists kept the beaches hopping and businesses boomed, but everything slowed down after Labor Day. We locals didn't mind the winter months, as most of us needed the time for revival.

Chapter Ten

IN MEMORIUM

One of the saddest days of my life began one morning when Dick Powell pulled into the parking lot and came into the shop. I was always happy to see him. On this day he told me he just wanted a quick trim as he was in a hurry. He was really hurting and needed to get out fast. I trimmed his hair and cleaned up the neck a little bit and I asked if there was anything I could do, to make him more comfortable. He said no, but he did want to talk to me. I had a premonition that something terrible was coming down because Dick was abnormally quiet. I offered to buy him a drink and we went over to Berkshire's and into the bar. He said, "Let's get a table in back. I have something to tell you and I'd rather talk in private." We went back to the far table and he said, "I just came from my doctor and the news was about as bad as it can get. I've just been informed that I have cancer and that I have three months left to live." I gasped, "Oh, God Dick, this cannot be!" I found I had no words to say. I was struck mute. I just couldn't believe what I had just heard. We sipped our drinks in silence for a short while and then he said, "Glenn, I don't mind going. I've had a hell of a good life. But I sure am going to miss those beautiful trips to Mexico and I always wanted to go up to Alaska in my boat." I immediately vowed that I'd scrape up a crew and if he wanted to make that trip to Alaska we would do it if he thought he was capable. I think it lit up his day a little bit. I wouldn't have given a second thought about closing up the shop and doing anything for this man, this friend of mine. He told me he really was in a hurry and he needed to get home to talk with his wife and kids. He was worrying about how he was going to tell his family and I assured him that by the time he got to Los Angeles he would know what to say and do. I tried to tell him how badly I felt for him but there really weren't any words to express my desolation. I watched him drive off and went back to the shop and told everyone that I was leaving for the day and to lock up for me. I'd see them in the morning. This day is permanently etched in my brain. It was just terrible.

In January 1963 my friend died. It was a terrible time for all that knew him. The news was in all the papers and other media. It was a sad day for the whole world because we lost one of the finest men I've ever had the pleasure of knowing. Rest in peace, old friend.

Chapter Eleven

ALL ABOUT "EVE"

On a much lighter note, I had a lot of great girlfriends in Newport Beach and I loved every one of 'em. They were fantastic women, great party gals and fun to be with. But then came a magic day when I met *the* one. I fell madly in love with her and the best part was that she fell madly in love with *me!* It was both good and bad that she was extremely famous, one of the biggest movie stars in the world. It was good for obvious reasons and bad because I simply felt that she was in a social class way beyond mine. It was the princess dating the commoner kind of thing. But we couldn't keep away from each other. I wasn't attracted to her for her fame…some of her pictures were a little sappy for my taste…it was only after I started getting to really know her that her incredible charisma and warmth made its impact on me.

I'd like to protect her identity from the casual reader so I'll just call her "Eve". I loved Eve so much that I sometimes felt sick when I couldn't be with her. She told me she felt the same way. She used to say that a day without Glenn was like a day without sunshine. It was not right that we continue our relationship and I knew that. It couldn't possibly go anywhere; there were just too many pitfalls in our path.

She had as much money as a small country, maybe more. She was adorable, famous and talented and the whole world loved her. She was the epitome of every bachelor's dream girl . . . and she loved little unknown Glenn Maxwell, the barber. Even married men who couldn't have her wanted to protect her and her career. Her husband had recently died and as she had loved him deeply, she was still mourning his death. I found her many times hiding in some room, crying her eyes out over something she had seen or heard, or maybe something someone would say that reminded her of him. I felt this was entirely understandable and I just felt sorry she had to go through her grieving period. I felt so badly for her. I would do anything to cheer her up. Fortunately I was good at this and it wouldn't take me too long to get her happy and laughing again. These incidents would break my heart and I wanted to kneel down beside her and cry for her heartache. But I couldn't do that. She had two young children, a 12-year-old boy and a girl a little over a year older than that. Somehow we became a team of four and traveled everywhere as a group. Wherever you'd find Eve and me, you'd know the kids were close at hand.

When I realized what was happening, that this was the real thing, I tried to show her how different my world was than hers. The two of us practically lived on the beach that year and she met my friends, who were not all celebrities by any means. But my friends now became her friends. We would play volleyball, baseball, have bonfires, sing, dance, take long walks at sunset, just about everything that you could do at the beach. We would go boating and fishing and just relax. The children loved it and so did I. She had a large home in Beverly Hills and another beautiful place in Newport Beach. She had homes in New York, Sun Valley, Idaho and other places as well.

I had a reason for not taking Eve out in the Hollywood area. It was a selfish reason. I knew that if we went out to dinner in one of her favorite restaurants in "her town", we would be opening up a huge can of worms. I was afraid of the gossip columnists who were very well known and carried a lot of weight in those days. They had the power to make or break careers. The two most feared ones were Louella Parsons and Hedda Hopper. Others that were well known were Walter Winchell and Harrison Carroll. Of course, there were many more than that, but the ones I mentioned by name come to my mind first after all these years.

These people could smell out a romance and it would make great copy, especially a story like ours . . . you know — MOVIE ROYALTY DATES BARBER. I didn't need this and besides, it was unheard of at the time. Things like that just didn't happen. It didn't matter if you were a *successful* barber. Even if you were a *millionaire* barber you just weren't in the class that could get away with wooing a movie star. You didn't *belong*. If these columnists liked you they would praise you to the skies but if they didn't approve of you they would skewer you like a fish and leave you gutted by the wayside.

Hollywood or not, we were extremely happy. Our love seemed to get stronger and stronger each and every day. It was so wonderful to see her happy and I basked in that happiness. She laughed a lot and would sing in the shower and around the house and it was good to hear the kids laughing so much. That was such a happy time and we all reveled in it and told each other so.

One fine day I ran into a friend of mine, Andy Anderson who was one of the owners of Knott's Berry Farm. This was way before Knott's became a giant theme park but at the time it was well known for being a great place for a home cooked chicken dinner and for the ghost town of Calico that they had recreated from the original buildings imported from the Mojave Desert. He owned a retreat up in the mountains at Big Bear Lake, a very pretty resort above the city of San Bernadino. He offered to let me use his place if I wanted to take my ladylove and the kids up there for a weekend. He told me we'd love it. I thanked him and he gave me a key and a map to show us the way.

It turned out to be a great trip up there. We left on Saturday morning and drove from Newport through Riverside and then started the winding trip up into the mountains. We drove up higher and higher until it seemed it was impossible to gain anymore altitude, which is when we arrived at the resort. We had made the trip fun by singing *Tea for Two* for about an hour. The girls would sing the girl parts and us two guys would chime in with the boy parts. Then just for fun we would reverse the parts with the guys doing the female lines. It was hilarious and we got a lot of laughs out of it.

Andy Anderson was absolutely correct. The resort and environs were breathtaking. There was a deck that encircled his hideaway. Looking out from it you felt you were on top of the world and I guess we were! The sunset that evening was remarkable, painted we felt, by

God, just for us. I barbecued steaks and we ate while watching the sunset. It was a marvelous hour. I remember Barbra Streisand softly playing on the stereo while we dined.

For some reason the kids were unusually quiet that evening. We could her them in the other room whispering and giggling. We wondered what they were up to but we just left them alone figuring they needed their privacy, too. After about an hour of this they came into the living room where we were. I glanced over and said, "What's up?" They asked us to sit down and listen to what they had to say because they had come to a decision. We did that and the children chorused, "Are you ready?" Yes, we were ready. "OK, we have decided that we want you two to get married." They were giggling but they weren't kidding, either. They really wanted me to be their new daddy. They said we all loved each other and they thought we would be a perfect family. I thanked them very much and assured them that yes, we really do love each other, but for me to marry their mother would be impossible. Almost in unison came the emphatic, "Why?" I went on to explain the facts of life and how difficult it would be to overcome the class barrier between their mother and myself. I tried to explain to them that their mother had great wealth and I did not and that everyone would think I was just marrying her for her money, which I would never do. Their mother was famous. I was not. Marriage to me would hurt her public image. Because their mother was a top movie star, she was in some ways, owned by the public and the public certainly loved her. By marrying me she could possibly loose her great popularity. Finally, I said that I could never be famous enough to be accepted by her millions of fans.

It was sad to see how disappointed and confused the children were. I asked them if we couldn't just love each other and enjoy each other while we could and that I would always be the best friend they ever had. I meant every word I said. It got very quiet and the children went to their room and went to bed. Eve and I didn't have much to say after that and a kind of sadness crept over the house. I went to bed but had a tough time falling asleep. I knew that what I wanted most in this life was just out of my reach and I couldn't stretch any further.

I didn't wake up the next day until almost noon. I could hear Eve and the kids downstairs laughing and sounding happy as could be. I jumped into the shower, shaved, brushed my teeth, got dressed and went down to join them. When I got down there the children looked at me and stared giggling and said, "Mom has something she wants to tell you and you'd better listen to it, mister." And then they ran outside.

I think I might have had an idea about what was coming and I poured a cup of coffee and sat down at the table with Eve. She looked at me for a long time, just staring into my eyes. I was not comfortable at all. Finally she spoke. "Are you in love with me, Glenn?" I replied, "You know very well how much I love you." She said, "Do you love the children?" and I said, "With all my heart." Then she said, "You just listen to me because I'm only going to say this once. I am a very rich person and what I do with my money is no one's business but mine. I earned it and I have the right to spend it any way I want to. I have enough money to last us five hundred years. If my career ended tomorrow, so what? So don't be using that as an excuse not to marry me. Don't I deserve to be happy? I have lived my life making the world happy making entertaining movies. Now it's my turn. And as far as my fans are concerned, I'm sure they will love you as I love you. What's not to love? I would rather spend one hour with you than with anyone else on Earth. Don't interrupt. I'm giving you two weeks. I'm going back east, to New York, and I'm going to do a big TV special and I'll just stay back there and never have to see you again if you decide to keep being so damned noble. My heart had come up in my throat and all I could do was kiss her. We held that kiss longer than any screen kiss ever filmed. I put everything into it, all my feelings and fears and it said everything I couldn't, for the life of me, say with words.

The days slowly passed and everyone I met was telling me how bad I looked and asked me if I was sick. They had no idea how sick I was. Inevitably, the days ticked away and the two weeks were almost up. She was leaving and so was my heart. Friday arrived, my deadline. I tried to keep my mind off Eve by running my business and staying as busy as possible. She had been chosen to make an appearance on a Perry Como special for *The Kraft Theater*. At the time this was one of the biggest and most prestigious programs on television. She would be doing the show live from Pittsburgh, Pennsylvania but most of the rehearsing would be in New York. At one time, Mr. Como had been a barber so at least we had something in common but that was small comfort.

The newspapers and TV news people and the rest of the media were now aware of our love affair and they were having a field day with the story. Every day some newspaper would come up with some stupid "will they or won't they" kind of thing. They were continually speculating about our plans and it was a constant irritation to both of us and I felt that it was another good reason for our little separation. I hoped that putting a continent between us might quiet the press down a bit, but it didn't. They kept the stories and rumors and gossip going and just wouldn't let go. When Eve left me and flew to New York I knew it would be the loneliest time of my life, and it was. Shortly before five on the next Friday the phone in the shop rang and my receptionist listened for a few seconds then looked up at me and said, "Glenn, I think you'd better take this in your private room on your private line." In the back office I found myself speaking to the producer of *The Kraft Theater*. He told me he was having a lot of trouble with Eve, that she hadn't been rehearsing well, she couldn't remember her lines, she was heartsick and I was the reason. They wanted me to drop everything and fly back and help Eve through the show. I was kind of shocked and told him, "You've gotta be kidding. Eve is a professional and she can do it. Just . . . " But he stood firm and wouldn't let me off the hook. So I asked if I might speak with Eve and when she came on the line she was crying and all upset and told me she just wasn't functioning well and she couldn't get her mind off me and wouldn't I·please, please make the trip so we could talk. What's a guy to do? I flew to New York.

I packed a little bag and drove to the airport feeling a combination of elation at the thought of seeing my sweetheart and confusion about our situation. As I entered the ticketing area to pick up the first class tickets the producers had arranged for me, I thought I was doing just fine. There was plenty of time to make the plane and I was thinking, "This is great! I've escaped the media at last" but no such luck. They were there all right, waiting at the gate. How do these things get out? Flashbulbs were popping and the TV news guys were sticking microphones in my face and asking me if I was flying back to tie the knot and all I would say was, "No comment, no comment, *no comment!*" I thought I would escape this insanity when I boarded the plane, but no! About ten reporters trooped onto my flight and I found myself begging them for a little privacy. I told them that I honestly didn't know *what* our plans were and I really had no comment so they might as well relax and enjoy the flight.

When the long trip ended and we finally landed in New York, Eve and her best friend, Carolyn Jones met me at the airport. I knew Carolyn, who starred in the TV show *The Addams Family*. She was married to Aaron

Spelling who went on to become one of the very biggest producers in the business. Both Carolyn and Aaron were wonderful people and good friends who would stick by you day and night.

When the reporters spotted Eve and Carolyn they went into another feeding frenzy. Were we really that important? I thought the whole scene was absolutely ridiculous. After the media circus, we were joined by an escort of airport officials and rushed to our waiting limo and made for the city. We had rooms at the Pierre Hotel on Fifth Avenue and after getting to our suite we sat up and talked the whole night through.

Carolyn remained with us and played the part of referee during our discussion. She knew her opinion meant a great deal to me. We went through the same old things about why we should or shouldn't get married and Carolyn could see we were so madly in love it was pitiful. She supported Eve by tell me that you only live once and we should take a shot at it. She said the world wouldn't stop turning and Eve's fans would certainly understand our romance and would go along with our decision. I just shook my head, knowing I was going to give in. I questioned Eve, "Do you love me?" She smiled, "Yes, I do." I then said, "Will you be my wife?" and she said, "If you want me I will." When Eve wanted something she got it, and this time she got me, Glenn Maxwell, barber. We were now engaged to be married. With Eve in a glow of happiness the rest of the rehearsals for the show went smoothly and shortly after that we proceeded to Pittsburgh for the final dress rehearsal. Her performance during the actual show was a smash, maybe the best performance she ever gave in her life. She got standing ovations as the audience went crazy over her. It was a triumph and we all felt relieved and wonderful, especially Perry Como who thanked me for saving the day. The producers thanked me. The sponsor thanked me. I felt like some sort of hero just for being with the woman that I loved.

After the show I was introduced to two marvelous people, Jerri and Paul Pollock, who had been with Eve for two or three days before I arrived. Apparently, the four of them, Jerri, Paul Carolyn and my fianceé, had been making plans. Now they took me aside and told me that all the arrangements had been made for all five of us to fly out that night for Miami Beach. Paul said, "When we get there you'll be staying in our best hotel." (Eve told me later that these nice folks had a gang of money and owned hotels all over the place and they were wonderful friends which, I had to agree, was certainly the truth). They told me the next day was going to very special and it certainly was. I was whisked off to Miami Beach an hour later and the fun was just beginning.

Paul met me early the next morning and took me to his barber. We then ate breakfast together. You see, this was my wedding day and Paul was my best man through the whole thing. Paul was making sure I was trimmed and well turned out. I guess I was looking good on the outside, but oh boy, inside I was as nervous as a long-tailed cat in a room full of rocking chairs.

We had to get special permission from the State of Florida to be married because there was a three day waiting period on the books and we just didn't want to wait that long. Eve had a tremendous amount of power and could pick up a phone and get just about anyone in the world she wanted to. In this instance she called a judge in Miami and he kindly waived the three-day requirement. He would also be marrying us and we were to be there by ten that morning.

I talked to the judge and he made it very clear that he didn't want a lot of reporters and news attention. He didn't want to be photographed or hassled in any way. He was emphatic about these things. I told him that I would do the best I could, but we really had no control over the press. When we left the hotel in the limo that morning I had to laugh. We were being tailed by at least a hundred cars. So much for no reporters and no publicity. I didn't mind. We were "the couple of the hour".

I had to laugh again when we arrived at the judge's home. No publicity? I couldn't believe this guy. He had even removed the first floor windows in his house so all the cameras would have a good shot at him. He was putting on a little show of his own! After the "I do's" were concluded we headed off through the hugs and kisses of our well wishers to a church where our marriage was blessed. But what a mad zoo. From the moment we left the hotel and for the rest of the day we were followed by a convoy of reporters and photographers and our every move was noted for their various news mediums. We were covered like a blanket. Our reception was held at the Pollock's home, an incredible place. It had marble floors that rambled up to a giant lawn that grew right down to the ocean. Tied up to their private dock was Paul's 140-foot yacht. Not bad, for an innkeeper!

The reception was a true gala. There were so many attending from all around the world that I couldn't help wondering if Eve hadn't planned this further in advance than I knew. But it sure was fun. Even my sister was there, having flown in from Northern California for the event.

Later that afternoon the children came down with Eve's private secretary. We had a real nice guy named Frank McFadden taking care of all the public relations. He was also our friend.

The whole thing was so romantic. When the sun began to set all the drapes were opened and I'll never forget this setting. It would have made a great painting. It was a long reception that didn't start thinning out until well after ten that night. It must have cost the Pollocks a fortune. Eve and I and the rest of the wedding party finally made our escape aboard Paul's beautiful yacht and set off in the direction of Cuba. On the way out someone made a suggestion that the yacht's captain should marry us again, "just to make sure it's legitimate". I didn't mind. Why not? I was enjoying everything to the hilt and that would make it three marriages in one day. It was a great day in my life and a fabulous night, too. We had a fine little cruise out in a calm ocean and didn't get back till three or four in the morning. We drove back to the hotel and finally we were alone. It had been a most hectic couple of days, but we survived them and it was time to start our lives together.

Here I was, an old married man again — at the age of thirty-one. The kids were ecstatic and wanted to stay in Miami Beach but they had to get back to school. Eve and I were anxious to fly home and get ready for a nice long honeymoon. We had talked about going to the Greek Isles but at that time there was a lot of unrest going on over there and we weren't so sure we wanted to be in the middle of it. Besides, we could go anywhere on Earth for our honeymoon and with the whole world to choose from it was a pleasantly tough decision to make. The phone was ringing and after Eve answered it I heard her say, "If you wait just a little while, I'll ask Glenn." She then asked my if I wanted to go to what she called "Shangri-la". I said, "Sure," even though I didn't have a clue as to its location or what its attraction was. Eve was more informed than I was and explained that it was very remote, and accessible only by boat or plane. There were no television sets, no newspapers, nothing but good food, romance, good music and beautiful company. The place was really named Palmilla and it was located in Baja, California.

So Palmilla was our choice and it was just the right place for us. We spent two weeks at a resort owned by Rod and Ed Rodriquez. Our plan was to get away without anyone knowing where we were. We would fly out of a private terminal in San Diego under the cover of darkness and by the time we got to Palmilla it would be daylight and everything would be peachy. This time everything worked to perfection and we left San Diego with Rod flying his own plane for us. Rod had some other guests on board and we started celebrating early and just had a great trip.

Palmilla is near the sea and is practically surrounded by fishing boats. The fishing was great and I managed to haul in several marlins and a few Dorados as well during our stay. The Dorado is as golden as its name. A beautiful, opalescent gold when it's alive, the Dorado can run over two or three feet in length. Unfortunately for the Dorado, he is delicious. The smaller marlins are returned to the sea, but not the tasty Dorado. The place was Seventh Heaven. I loved it and so did Eve. We had much private time to ourselves and enjoyed every minute we spent there. I don't think the Greek Islands could have been any better for our honeymoon but we planned to go there someday soon. Now that I think about it, we never did get to the Greek Isles.

Because there weren't even any telephones in Palmilla, nothing and nobody could disturb us. We always woke up late in the morning and ate breakfast in the beautiful dining room. There was excellent food and a relaxing atmosphere there. The rest of the time we did anything our hearts desired. Besides the fishing, swimming and horseback riding, we could take a little pleasure jaunt on one of the boats or maybe just a romantic walk on the virgin beach. When we felt like going out on the water, Rod would loan us a little boat he had and we'd cruise around the harbor to our hearts' content.

I will never forget those heavenly evenings. I could spend a year dreaming about perfect romantic nights and not come up with anything better than what we had. Rod was always importing different Mariachi bands. They came from Cabo San Lucas, Mazatlan and if they were good enough, even as far away as Acapulco and Puerto Vallarta. After dinner, whatever band that happened to be working that particular night would come around and start playing beautiful romantic Spanish music like *Besa Mi Mucho* and *La Noche de Ronda*, every one dripping with romance. Eve and I would dance and take walks on the beautifully laid out paths that crisscrossed the resort. They were subtly lighted so you could see the flowers and waterfalls and citrus trees. The Mariachis would follow us so that we had music wherever we went. Even when we turned in we'd hear the band out there singing these romance-filled songs. I really enjoyed that. Maybe in another life I was a Mariachi. It really is fortunate that I love that kind of music because we sure got enough of it!

And so the idyllic two weeks passed all too quickly and it was time to get back to the real world and to business. We also had been talking about buying a new house in Newport Beach and we wanted to get started on that project. But most of all, we wanted to see the kids who we were starting to miss something awful.

Chapter Twelve

FROM THE PINNACLE TO THE PITS

We said our farewells in Palmilla and before we knew it we were back in San Diego where we were met by our chauffeur and driven up to Los Angeles. Back home, things started moving at warp speed. We had numerous meetings with Eve's agency and business managers. We finalized our decision to buy a home on Lido Island that we had walked through before our honeymoon. I'd be able to stroll to my shop every day if I wanted to. The home was being offered by Milton Bren and his wife, actress, Claire Trevor. The house was a real showplace and had been built by Milt's son, Donald who had become a well-known builder in the Newport Beach area. Donald and I had been friends for years and he had been discharged from the Marines about the same time I was released from the service.

It was a gem of house and had been designed mostly by Claire who was also an artist. Her paintings were delightful and her home was almost like a gallery. The upstairs bedroom opened up and looked down on the living room and you could see all of her paintings from there. The ceilings were very high and airy and Eve and I could hardly wait to move in.

My wife had gotten a call from Harold Kennedy, a producer in New York. He had written a play and named it *Goodbye Ghost*. He wanted to take it out as a summer stock production and wanted Eve to play the lead. Eve got all excited because there were roles for two children in it. It was a comedy. Eve asked the kids if they would like to spend their summer working in the show. Would they! Even I was offered a job as assistant to the producer so the entire family was "going on the road".

We went to New York for rehearsals and opened the play in a small town called Sullivan, which is in Illinois. From there we took the show to Indianapolis, Denver, Pheasant Run (outside Chicago), Connecticut, Kennebunkport in Maine, Tapensy in New York and then to Palm Beach, Florida. That was quite a tour, folks. The play was highly successful and Eve and the kids had fun doing it. As for me, I got a good show business education and made a little money as well. Eve, being professional at all times, played to packed houses throughout the run. All of us hated to see it end.

Before returning to California, it seemed like a perfect time to take a breather for a little while and since we were so close, we ended up in the Grand Bahamas, off the Florida coast. After a week of R and R we went back to Newport. There was still a little summer left and we thought the kids might like a little trip to top off their vacation. We told them we would take them anywhere they felt like going and we were secretly delighted when they decided they would rather stay right there in beautiful Newport Beach.

We made the move into our new Lido Island home. The kids were all jazzed because they were looking forward to going to school in Newport, and I was excited because I had begun to think of Newport Beach as my hometown. Eve was as happy as a clam at high tide because she had so many show business friends in the area. We were all one happy and satisfied little family.

Now one does not move into a grand house like ours without some help and I don't mean just the moving people. Eve hired the famous decorator, Andy Gearhart to design the interior and shape the decor. We had decided we wanted nothing but happy hues like green and yellow and white in every room and we wanted this color scheme to run right into the courtyard, which was a showplace in itself. The entire house was surrounded by a twelve-foot fence. Guests had to be electronically buzzed into the courtyard. A giant door, which was the house's main entrance, would open to allow entry. We even had a little freshwater moat encircling the place.

Andy and Eve did such a great job that the house won and award from *Home and Garden* magazine. To celebrate the award and to "christen" our little castle, we decided to have a housewarming party.

Thinking back, it was not unusual to see Eve, the kids and me in the newspaper and on television. For two solid years there was always something about us *Photoplay, Modern Screen, Motion Pictures* and all the other movie magazines that were so popular at the time. I don't think Harrison Carroll *ever* left us out of his column. Sometimes his entire piece was about us and what we were up to. Thanks, Harrison for writing only nice things and being so kind to us. Coverage like this informed the world what we were doing at all times. It didn't bother me that much because at that time all was rosy, but when changes started happening . . . well, I'll be getting to that later.

Housewarming day arrived. We had invited all our friends in Newport Beach and I don't know how many invitations went out to Beverly Hills, Hollywood, Los Angeles and other bastions of the entertainment industry. All we wanted to do was introduce all of our Newport friends to the other friends that Eve had enjoyed for years. We wanted to get them all together, get to know one another and have a good time. Well, folks started arriving around seven that night. The house was filling up but I couldn't help noticing that most of our guests were locals and there were only a few coming down from the city where most of the invitations had gone. I thought that was strange, especially since Carolyn and Aaron didn't show. Oh, well, the people who were there were having a good time and Eve didn't seem to mind, which goes to show what a good actress she is. It really was some grand wingding, not only extending into the wee hours but past them. The bash started Saturday evening and we ended up serving breakfast to about forty tuckered out fun-timers on Sunday morning!

Eventually, we had our house back to ourselves and things got to back normal. As for the people we'd invited that didn't make it down from Los Angeles, I reasoned that it was a hundred-mile round-trip for them and who knew why they had chosen not to come? There were probably a lot of other parties that night that were closer to home for them, or maybe some of them just weren't party people; I didn't think a whole lot about it although I was glad we had sent out the invitations. But Eve was thinking about it a lot. She knew she had been snubbed for the first time in her life.

Saying she was disturbed is putting it mildly. For the next few days she was very quiet and moody. There was no way I could sit her down and talk to her or cheer her up or anything. She spent a lot of time, almost the whole week, on the telephone in long conversations with some of the very people in the city who had let her down. I didn't really know what was happening, but I felt a cold chill up my back and I knew something was going wrong.

About a week after that, I came home to find Eve in her dressing room behind a locked door. I knocked softly to let her know I was back from work. She said she'd be out in just a little while. I went into my office and noticed a half-opened envelope on my desk that hadn't been there that morning. Although the letter was addressed to Eve, the letter was sticking half out of the envelope and my curiosity got the better of me. Normally we didn't read other's mail unless invited to do so but I couldn't help myself. Was this the cause behind that locked door?

I will not dignify the writer of the letter by giving you his name. He's been dead for a long time, anyway. He made his living as a ventriloquist and had two dummies that I still feel must have been smarter and kinder than he was. Here is what this "funny" fellow wrote to my Eve:

Dearest Eve,

I am sorry, but as you know I have been knighted by the King of Sweden and I do not deem it proper to associate with a barber.

I think that this started something in my mind. It hurt a lot, an awful lot, and I wondered to myself what if Eve's name had been Mary and I was a carpenter. Would this utter ass have felt the same way? I believe he would have.

The days, the weeks, the months went by and I still couldn't cheer up my Eve. Of course I was worrying that my worst nightmare was coming true. I had predicted this very sort of thing. Her fans didn't seem to hate me, but coming from someone she had considered her friend, this kind of trash was too much for her. I loved her. I didn't ever want to destroy what she had before she met me. I felt it all closing in on me and I hated what this one unkind note was doing to our marriage. The fact that I was responsible for hurting her in any way drove me up a wall. So I started drinking more and we started arguing more.

I think that subconsciously I was trying to drive her into giving me up. I knew I couldn't walk away, but maybe she would kick me out and the only way I could get her to call it a marriage and agree to a divorce was to actually run her into a corner. Please don't get me wrong. Eve is not the kind of person that would go that far just because a few people she thought were her friends had proven different. The majority of the folks I met along the way were great and they accepted me and liked me. They were big enough to accept me into their worlds and their families. But then this one guy . . . I don't know. As I said, I began drinking harder and arguing louder. I don't think Eve was even aware that I might have been hurt more than she was by this moron. And there I was, hanging out with my Newport buddies, the life of the party, staying out half the night and coming home drunk. In my mind I felt I had to drive her away from me to the point of a divorce because I really felt that would be the best thing for her.

But she kept putting up with me. One of our wedding anniversaries was coming around. Instead of going out we decided it would be nicer to stay home and have a quiet dinner with the kids. After dinner we could sip some fine wine and have a serious conversation. Eve and I had already exchanged gifts and she had given something really nice to me and I was touched. And then the kids gave me their gift (which I treasure to this day) and it completely changed my thinking. It was a gold St. Christopher medal and on the back had been engraved, "To the best Dad in the world." It was signed with their names. I'd forgotten that the kids loved me, too. I couldn't chase Mom away without losing them along with her. They would be hurt and in their innocence it wouldn't be fair. I realized that I'd better look a little farther ahead on this path of destruction that I was taking.

By this time the news media had gotten wind of our troubles at home. They seemed to know every word we said to each other and if they didn't, they'd just make up something. But it's really incredible what reporters can ferret out when they have their noses into a story. I guess it's about a thousand percent worse today. It was as though they had spies in every corner and every argument Eve and I had would somehow surface in the papers or some magazine almost every night there would be some unhappy reference to us on TV. It became a vicious circle. The bad things we were seeing and hearing just led to more and more arguing and fighting within our family. It was terrifying for me, as I was really just a very ordinary person and not looking for publicity of any kind and certainly not the kind of garbage I was seeing, even if there was a kernel of truth in it.

Eve was looking forward to a television show her agent had booked in Los Angeles. Two of her best friends were also going to be in it, Judy Garland and Steve Lawrence. In fact, it was Judy's own program, *The Judy Garland Show*. Eve and I stayed about three days in the city while she rehearsed. It must have been the night before the show that we got into an awful argument about something that I can't even remember now. I didn't want to be around that scene anymore and I certainly didn't want to be upsetting Eve's rehearsals or fouling up the show in any way. And I didn't want to hurt her feelings any more than I already had. I left the car and driver with Eve and hitchhiked back to Newport Beach. (This was before serial killers roamed the streets.) It wasn't very long until a car full of Marines on their way to San Diego picked me up. They were kind enough to detour into Newport and we stopped at a local tavern and I stood a few rounds. Then they left, four happy Marines leaving behind one unhappy Glenn. I called a friend who came to pick me up and I made my way home.

What I'd started had borne fruit, and despite my second thoughts, Eve wasn't to happy with me and had had about all of me she could stand. We decided we had better split up and we did. It was a bad time. It was a sad time. The divorce came through and the press went crazy, you know the drill by now. I thought to myself that it had been a nice ride and it was over. Never mind that I missed Eve terribly. I didn't contest anything and asked for nothing in the divorce proceedings. I told my lawyer to give her anything she wanted and to just make sure she was happy. She could start a new life afresh without me

After our divorce, Eve moved back up to L.A. and I remained in Newport. My best friend had become the bottle. I'd wake up and drink, drink all through the day and all night. Then I'd wake up and do it again. I was going downhill as fast as I possibly could. My spirit was so down. Every night I'd watch the news with weary eyes and there would be some reference to *her*. I'd think, "That's my wife . . . that's *not* my wife." There was nothing unusual about her press coverage. It had been that way before I'd ever met her. She drew media attention wherever she went. Meanwhile, I was having a tough time pulling myself back together. I was working a little bit here and there, but I really couldn't put my heart into anything. I really felt that my life had probably ended at that point and I just didn't give a damn about anything or anyone. I was in this limbo-like world for about a year.

I must be a glutton for punishment. I'd always watch anything that came on TV about my ex-wife. One night a story popped up telling the world that she was going to marry again. I happened to know this guy and I couldn't stand the man. He was a total phony. He made a career out of finding lonely rich women and they would support this leech until they grew to really know him and he would move on to his next mark. I was livid. I hadn't talked to Eve in quite awhile and I'm sure I had no right to do what I did, but I didn't care. Eve was still Eve, a warm, sweet wonderful person. I wanted more for her than this. I called her on the phone and her secretary told me to leave a number where I could be reached and she would call me back. I really didn't think she would, but she did.

After doing a little personal catch up on our lives I practically shouted, "Good God, lady! Do you think I let you go just so you'd wind up marrying some creep like ____? I really chewed her out, up one side and down the other. She listened, not saying a word. She told me she had sort of missed me. One thing led to another and she asked me if I could come up and join her for a quiet dinner in her penthouse apartment in West Los Angeles. Of course I would. Two weeks later we were remarried. Here we go again!

In the first year of ours new marriage we did a lot of things. We traveled a lot, in the States and around the world. I didn't know it, but I was traveling in "high society", known eventually as the "jet setters". During these days I met some of the most celebrated people of the times. Eve knew more people in high places than you could ever imagine. Even I didn't believe it until I found myself actually being introduced to these international names, names that I'd only read about before my marriage to Eve. Starting with the President of the United States on down, she knew them all and they all loved her. And there was nothing they wouldn't do for her. There I was, smack-dab in the middle of more money and power than I could have dreamed, and it was all because of Eve.

We traveled and enjoyed ourselves. Neither of us was doing much work — we were too busy just being together. It was sort of a huge second honeymoon. Finally back in Newport Beach, one of my old wishes became reality. Remember that boat I lusted for? It was mine for the asking and it wasn't just any old boat, either. She was black with gold trim and ketch-rigged — the most beautiful motor sailing boat I had ever laid eyes on. She was just what I used to dream about and now I owned her. *Marco Polo* was her name. Of course it wasn't just for me. Our whole family spent a lot of happy times on this floating dream of mine, in fact so much time that sometimes it felt like we were practically living on her.

But sometimes I would find myself alone with her, just me and my boat. On one such solo cruise I met a unique little character that was unlike anyone I've met before or since.

Chapter Thirteen

MR. "P" AND MR. "X"

Two of the most remarkable things happened to me during the time that I owned the Marco Polo. I fondly remember Mr. "P" and Mr. "X". I now share these stories with you.

I remember one night I was returning home from a trip I'd made to Ensenada in Baja, California. I was alone on my boat because those that were with me on this particular voyage had flown home from San Diego and the young man that I had hired, as my deck hand had not shown up. I had to get the boat back to Newport Beach because Eve and I were leaving for New York City the following week. I didn't like the idea of sailing her home alone, I but felt that I could safely make it.

I left San Diego Harbor about 5:00 p.m. There was a lot of daylight left as it was summertime and I started up the coast to Newport. Wonders can happen when you are at sea, alone with your thoughts. First and foremost, I'm thinking about the boat—the sea conditions such as the wind and current, setting the sails and so on. When this is all taken care of a person can relax and truly enjoy the voyage.

The winds were down and I was under power. My boat the Marco Polo was powered by Mercedes Benz Diesel engines, and I decided for safety reasons, that I would go out to sea, set my course and put the boat on automatic pilot.

Dusk came quickly and the purple hue of the sky became the dark blue of the night. I went below and turned on my running lights and the cabin lights. As I said, it was summertime, and it was warm and comfortable. It was a magic night. As I looked back at the wake of the boat, the whole sea lit up as if I was towing a giant florescent light behind me. Every wave was alive and lit up as it crashed into the next wave. The reason for this is the plankton in the water that gives the sea a florescent glow that is breathtakingly beautiful. You almost feel as though you are in another world.

It was about 10:00 p.m. and I was at the wheel, checking the compass heading when heard this strange noise up near the bow of the boat. I turned on my spreader lights to find out what was going on.

I walked up to the bow and couldn't believe at what I was looking at—Out of the night sky had come a very large bird—a pelican—and it had landed on the deck of my boat.

I looked at him and he looked at me and for some reason I started laughing and said, "Welcome aboard, Mr. Pelican—make yourself at home." I didn't want to scare him away because he really looked tired and beat up.

I went back to the steering area and made a small correction on the autopilot and went below and opened a large bag of spicy Dorito chips. I then went up to Mr. Pelican and gave him one of the chips. He seemed to like it. Then I walked back to the stern of the boat and I left a path of chips to the helm where I piloted the boat.

Within ten minutes that bird ate his way right beside me. I looked at him and he looked at me and that was the beginning of a beautiful friendship.

I started talking to him in a soft voice and said things, such as, "I wonder how long you've been flying and I wonder where you have been. I wonder where you started from and why you are here? I told him he had permission to explore the boat and he could stay as long as he wished and that I would understand if he felt he had to leave.

The strange thing was that every time I would talk to him he would turn his head and look at me as if he could understand every word I was saying.

I went below and opened a can of beer. I poured half of it into a soup bowl and placed the bowl down by Mr. "P", as I had decided to call him. I drank my half of the can of beer and he started drinking his half and he really seemed to like and appreciate the stuff. I also laid some more chips beside him.

After he drank his beer and ate his chips he walked down into the living quarters of the boat. I turned on all the inside lights so he could see better and he walked around as if he were inspecting the ship. He then came out on deck and walked up to the bow on the port side of the boat and returned on the starboard side and then hopped up and sat right beside me. This really surprised me. Here was this wild, free and very large bird sitting right beside me acting as tame as the punch at a church social. I even started petting him and he seemed to enjoy it. I was deeply touched by this and silently in awe of our connection to each other.

Now that I am older and looking back on this, I wonder if God sent me an Angel in the form of this large bird to keep me company. Did He know that I was a little nervous about being out at sea all alone and it being so late at night? Maybe God had sent "the Comforter". Thank You, Father God.

Mr. "P" and I shared another bag of chips along with another can of beer and before long I could see the buoy outside the Newport Beach jetty. It is always lit at night to assist boats in navigating to the entrance to the harbor.

It was now about 1:00 a.m. and as we entered the channel, Mr. "P" was out on the bowsprit admiring all the beautiful lights of Newport Harbor. I couldn't believe he had not flown away, but was expecting him to leave any minute, hoping all the while that he wouldn't as I was enjoying his company so much.

It was breathtaking coming into Newport Harbor that night with all the lights reflecting on the water. That night the water was a smooth as glass. A very gentle breeze was blowing and the air seemed so clean and fresh. It had been the best trip one could ask for.

After finding my mooring I slowly and carefully pulled *The Marco Polo* into her slip and stepped off onto the dock. I secured the bowlines and then went aft and secured the stern lines. Then I came back aboard and shut down the engines. I then hooked up the telephone lines and plugged in the dockside electricity. Lastly, I went through the boat and straightened everything up. Now all that was left to do was turn out all of the lights and the *Marco Polo* was secured for the night. Oh God, how I loved that boat. She was so beautiful - her gleaming, black hull and gold trim and her glistening, white decks and the mahogany masts made her something to see.

Now, I had to think about my newfound shipmate, Mr. "P". Did he want to bunk down aboard the boat or should I take him home with me? I decided to call Eve and let her know I was home safe and sound and then I told her that I might be bringing a houseguest with me, but to tell the maid not to makeup the guestroom. She laughed and asked me where did I expect my guest to sleep and I replied, "In the courtyard." and I hung up the phone. I chuckled to myself about what must be going through her mind. I finished securing the boat and started walking up the ramp to my car. When I got to the top of the ramp, I looked back and Mr. "P" was right on my tail.

He walked up to the car with me and I opened the car door on the passenger side and he just stared at me, so I reached down and picked him up and set him gently on the seat. I was expecting that this would make him very nervous, but no, he just seemed to settle down, no problem at all.

My house was only about a ten-minute drive from the boat, so we were home very quickly.

Mr. "P" didn't seem to mind the ride at all. He just sat there looking out the window.

When I got home, I parked the car in the garage. I opened the passenger side of the car and waited to see what Mr. "P" would do. I was expecting to lift him out of the car, but no, he just hopped out and I walked over to the side door, leading into the kitchen and he walked right in the house with me.

Eve and the kids had stayed up because they were worried about me being alone on the boat and they were wondering what kind of a guest I would bring home. They were fully expecting to see a man and then they got a look at Mr. "P". *Huh?*

I then proceeded to tell them the story of this bird and me. We all got a good laugh out the story. My family just loved him. It was really late and I was starting to feel really tired. I put Mr. "P" out in the courtyard for the night so that in case he wanted to fly away he could.

But here was the part I was concerned about. We had this big German Shepherd whose name was Willie. I didn't know if the two of them would get along, but I found out that Mr. "P" could take care of himself quite nicely. Willie didn't know what to make of him and Mr. "P" seemed to let Willie know that he wouldn't take any guff.   Amazing! I knelt down and petted Willie with one hand and petted Mr. "P" with the other and they seemed to accept each other.

I was tired, as I said before and needed some sleep. I told my family that I just had to bring Mr. "P" home with me or they would never have believed my story, and then we all went to get some sleep. I also told them not to be disappointed if he flew away during the night.

Surprise! When I woke up, I heard a lot of laughing going on out in the courtyard. I looked out of my bedroom window and there was Eve, the kids, the maid and the butler, and Willie and Mr. "P" chasing each other around. Mr. "P" had found a loving home. Eve and the kids fell in love with him just as I had.

This was on a Friday and I had promised my family that I would take them to Catalina Island the next day. I woke up Saturday morning and after a quick breakfast I started loading the car with food and drink for the trip to Catalina.

After the supplies were all loaded up, Eve and the kids got in my car and the maid and butler got in the station wagon and I went to get Mr. "P" in the courtyard. He had been there all day Friday, but now, oh boy—he was *gone!* I went back to the car and told them Mr. "P" had left us. We all felt a little sad that he was missing, but, as Eve explained to the kids, maybe he had a family, too and maybe missed them and flew away to his home.

I had to stop at the market on the way to the boat. I wanted to barbecue steaks that night in Catalina and I needed some more things but we got to the boat within an hour and everyone grabbed something and carried it down to the boat.

When we got aboard and put the supplies away, I fired up the engines and backed out of the slip and slowly went up the harbor to the jetty and out to sea. It was another perfect summer day, just right for our trip. It was warm, with gentle breezes and smooth seas—you couldn't ask for better sailing conditions.

But as we went out past the buoy, I heard Eve let out a scream! The reason Eve had screamed was because she had been sunbathing, lying on her back, very relaxed, and she had her eyes closed, enjoying the sun when Guess Who came in for a loud landing right beside her. Now when a pelican lands, it just drops soundlessly from the sky, so many feet from where it is going to land. Pelicans land with a thud and immediately start flapping their wings, which are very long, wide and large, to balance themselves. Mr. "P" landed right beside Eve and she didn't see him or hear him coming and then when she heard that loud thud, immediately followed by flapping these huge wings over her, she was nearly scared to death. Poor Eve. But how on earth had he found us? Who was this wonderful creature?

We all had a great time that weekend, lying in the sun, swimming, and barbecuing steaks with all the trimmings. Mr. "P" would dive off the mast of the boat and catch a fish and show it to all of us before he ate it. Incredible!

How nice it was to have the whole family together. That night we broke out the ukeleles and bongo drums and sang Calypso songs and seafaring ditties. It was great fun and the time went by too quickly.

On Sunday afternoon, we had to leave Catalina, and head for home as we had to get ready for out trip to New York City the next day. We hated to leave. We got back to Newport with no problems. I pulled the boat into the slip, secured it and double-checked all the lines. After it was all secured, we were ready to head for home. All except Mr. "P". We watched him fly up to the top of the main mast of the boat and land on the spar and bid us farewell. We all followed him with our eyes as he flew out to sea maybe to his home and family wherever they might have been. God bless him.

We all stood there waving goodbye to Mr. "P". We watched until we couldn't see him anymore. I looked at Eve and saw a tear running down her cheek. We all reluctantly got in the car. It was a quiet ride home. We were all crushed inside that our new friend had to leave us, but I couldn't leave my family like this, so I said, "Eve, darling, you have made a career out of waving goodbye to people flying away from you."

Of course we all laughed and started recounting all the movies she had made with scenes at airports, watching her "loved one" fly away with a tear in her eye. It put everyone in a better mood and we all lightened up. We knew that Mr. "P" had to do what he had to do and being free was one of his choices.

As for Mr. "P", thanks Buddy, for being such a good companion when I really needed you to keep me company. Thank you for bringing such joy to my family. Wherever you are, this world or the next one, I wish you God's speed.

***

Now it's time to share with you my story about Mr. "X". Our Mr. "X" was a dolphin that I became friends with. We were going out to sea again on another beautiful day and as we were leaving Newport Harbor, a school of dolphins surrounded our boat and started playing and swimming. I was at the helm, steering the boat and eating a ham and cheese sandwich. In my excitement to get a better look at the dolphins, I threw the ham and cheese sandwich up in the air, into the ocean. Before it fell into the water, one dolphin came out of the water and caught the sandwich in the air and ate it! I guess he liked it because he stayed with me a long time that day and he ate three more ham and cheese sandwiches.

I named him Mr. "X" because on his forehead he carried a large scar, probably from getting hit by the propeller of a boat. The scar was shaped like an "X".

What a riot this guy was. He seemed to hang around the buoy just outside the jetty. When he would spot my boat he would just porpoise out of the water, leaping high into the air until he got to my boat and, of course, I would have a ham and cheese sandwich ready to throw to him.

For almost three months, every time I took the *Marco Polo* out of the harbor, he would be waiting for me and I always had his ham and cheese sandwiches for him.

I think there was something about that boat that made the birds and the fish feel safe and at peace when they were around it - or maybe they felt my love for them and in their way they were returning that love. I'd like to believe that.

Eve and I and the kids had many happy hours aboard that beautiful boat and I shall never forget those days, ever.

As for you, Mr. "X", I hope that wherever you are, this world or the next, that you have found happy seas and you are having the best time that any dolphin could possibly have. God bless you, dear friend. And thank you for all the joy you brought to my family and me.

Chapter Fourteen

ANOTHER FAILURE

Unfortunately, the sailing was not all that smooth for Eve and me. Even though we had reconciled, I was firmly into the drinking habit and the arguments seemed to be just another bad habit that neither of us could overcome. In fact, there came a time when it seemed we were just tolerating each other. What was happening? Where did that wild love go? I don't suppose I'm the first person to ask that question, but our second marriage ended up the same way as the first, in the divorce court. Was it my fault? Mostly yes. But we both had our personal gremlins and I don't wish to rehash my side of the story in these pages. Let's just say we were both happy that the endless fighting was finally over with and leave it at that.

Our second marriage had all the ups and downs either of us could handle. Obviously there were more downs than ups but I must say that through this wonderful lady I met a myriad of the greatest people in the world. I associated with, and even campaigned with Presidents. I dined at the White House. I was in a strata of society that most anyone would enjoy being, and right here I'd like to thank Eve for all the interesting people she made possible for me to meet and all the fascinating places we visited. It was through her that I got to the "top of the mountain" and planted my flag there, complete with my name on it. The good times were awesome and the bad times were miserable, not only for the two of us but for the children, too. The kids were terribly hurt by our second break-up and for this I am deeply sorry. In my heart they will always remain "my kids" even though they are now middle-aged adults.

In over 25 years there has not been a single contact between Eve and me. She remarried and from what I see in the papers from time to time, she seems to be a very happy lady and I'm glad for her. I've never wished anything for her but the best and there will always be a special place in my heart for her and "my kids".[1]

---

[1] Eve's real name is no secret and all of you who remember the torrent of publicity we received, good and bad will know exactly who she is. If you don't know, it really isn't important. I'm not writing this to glorify her or myself, I'm writing to glorify God. The only reason I've mentioned it at all is to let you know that at one time in my life, for better or worse, I reached the pinnacle of material success. Also, the other celebrities I've mentioned are deceased but Eve is very much alive.

Chapter Fifteen

FLASHBACK

As you now know, I arose from humble beginnings, got to the top of the mountain and then fell off in a big way, taking a wrenching free-fall back to anonymity. You might say I was no worse off than I had been before my wild ride with Eve, but that wouldn't be true. Even though Eve was no longer a part of my life I was not really anonymous at all. That fact, plus my increased dependence upon alcohol worked against me.

I stuck around Hollywood for a year or so after the divorce and became a well-known "party animal". I couldn't get enough beautiful women, booze and general revelry. My status as Eve's ex-husband seemed to attract all sorts of characters. Complete strangers would buy me drinks and some even thought that I had access to Eve's money and could help them out in business deals. Everyone seemed to know that I was connected to plenty of other famous folks besides Eve and I was welcomed all over the place. I would string along the people who thought I could help them do business with Eve, even though I had no intention in the world of bothering her about any of them. I was just having fun — wasn't I? Sadly, I really wasn't.

The Hollywood scene got pretty stale after awhile and it certainly wasn't the same without Eve. Looking back, I can see that I was really a lost soul. I knew I should stop drinking so much, but what then? I thought drinking was essential to the social whirl. What would life be like without women and parties? I had no desire to get off that particular merry-go-round. My biggest problem was that I couldn't stand to be by myself. When I was alone, little awful thoughts would creep into my mind about my life and what had become of it. My solution to this problem was to avoid being by myself at all costs. Hey, go to another party! Live it up and drink to oblivion. Repeat as soon as possible. Who knew that I was suffering inside? I was always looking good, smiling and laughing — the life of any party no matter where it was. The reality - I was not having a good time at all.

I bless the fact that God has a way of stepping in when you are in this kind of mental and physical bind. It is said that God works in mysterious ways and for me His help began with a serious health problem. I had no idea this problem would eventually become a solution, but it did. You'll understand why a little later, but for now I'll continue with my story.

* * *

I had to have a hip replacement due to an injury I had received during my Korean War years. The procedure had just become available and I was one of the first patients to receive this new surgery. I was hospitalized for almost a full month. It was a very painful operation and I wasn't too enthused when I was told that my other hip would need to be replaced within a year. But this was just the beginning. Nine months later I developed a cancerous tumor on my right leg bone just above my knee. My doctor told me I would need more surgery as quickly as possible and that if the tumor ruptured during the operation that my leg would have to be amputated on the spot to save my life. There was about a sixty-percent possibility this would happen. I began to think that I was getting some sort of retribution for all the "fun" I was having.

Mulling over this new development I came to the conclusion that all in all I had lived a pretty wonderful life up to this point. If the leg had to go, or even if I died on the operating table, I'd done most everything I had ever dreamed possible and although I was only forty-one years old, if I didn't make it, so be it. But

God reached out and put His hand on me. He showed me that there was much more for me to experience that was clean, decent, fun, funny, exciting and every other positive adjective in the English language.

* * *

Now it never entered my mind that I would ever love any other woman as much as I had loved Eve. How wrong I was. To begin the story about my Sally, I have to go back in time. I was 28 years old and she was 27. I was working at the Shaving Mug on Lido Island. I always arrived for work a half an hour early at eight-thirty in the morning. The shop opened at nine. The shop front was all windows from floor to ceiling. It looked into the lobby of the attached building and was a three-story professional building. In the lobby, on the ground floor, was a small gift shop and coffee shop named the Blue Dolphin. It was a great coffee shop and noted for its good food and homemade pies that were topped by about two inches of real whipped cream. The front and back of the building were made of heavy glass so I could see who were coming and going into the building and also who was coming and going in and out of the coffee shop.

Well, it was on a bright and beautiful morning in March of 1961. A young lady stepped out from the passenger side with her back to me. As she leaned over to pick up her purse, I could see she had long light brown hair and the sides were pulled up into a ponytail. The ponytail part was very sun-bleached and the rest of her hair hung down her back. The sun just caught the sun-bleached part and it seemed to radiate light. She turned around I felt my heart go flip-flop. She was beautifully dressed and wore immaculate white gloves. She did not look to the left or to the right and carried herself like a princess. Her posture was superb. I just lost my breath. I thought she was the sweetest and most lovely girl I had ever seen. She was so feminine and appealing to me that I found myself speechless. That's really something for me.

It turned out that it was her first day at work as a legal secretary on the third floor of the building. Old "Silver Tongue" here was struck dumb every time I saw her and I saw her about she five times each day. It was a full two months before I got up the nerve to ask her to have coffee with me on her afternoon break. Unfortunately, I had asked a friend to come along and he monopolized the whole conversation. About all I managed to get out was, "I'm sorry, but I have to get back to work." At least I had learned her name, Sally. She was very apologetic about not talking to me and I asked her if we might have coffee again sometime. She said she would enjoy that very much and we both went back to work. But it seemed as if fate was against me because after that, every time I saw her go into the Dolphin I had a customer in my chair and couldn't leave the shop. We did begin waving to each other as she waited for the elevator, but we never had a conversation.

I found out that she had a younger brother who was half of a well-known comedy team in the Newport Beach area. The duo was known as "Skiles & Henderson" and Pete Henderson was her brother. His partner, Bill Skiles, had been a few years ahead of Sally at Newport Harbor Union High School. The comedy team was appearing at a place next to Balboa Island called The Villa Marina and they were packing them in every night. Not only were they funny, they were also superb musicians, each one playing several instruments and vocalizing as well.

There was a small dance floor where you could dance between the shows and a beautiful large round bar with a big pillar. The pillar was filled with water and live fish in front of the stage. The place also had a lovely restaurant and two show rooms. Pete and Bill played in the lounge. I went to the Villa almost every weekend to see if Sally was there and she usually was. She would either be with a date, with girlfriends or her mother. Sally liked to dance and when she and her date went out on the dance floor, I would take my date on the floor and try to maneuver over to dance next to Sally. We would exchange a few words and she was always friendly and smiling. She seemed genuinely happy to see me. After about a month she asked me if I cut women's hair. I told her that I did. This was on a Saturday night. She asked if she could make a hair appointment during her lunch hour on the following Tuesday. I was delighted with this development and said, "Sure!"

Next Tuesday Sally appeared right on time. As I combed out her very long hair she couldn't help notice that my hands were shaking pretty badly. She noticed this and said. "Tell me the truth. You've never cut a woman's hair before, have you?" I had to confess that indeed I had not. She said that was O.K. and all she wanted me to do was take off about a quarter of an inch all the way around and to take my time and relax. What she couldn't see was how badly my knees were shaking! Well, I followed her advice and took my time and trimmed her hair the way she had asked. I would have done her hair free of charge but René, the owner was running the cash register and so I had to ask her to pay him. She did so and came back to the chair and gave me a tip and thanked me. I felt terrible about having to ask her to pay anything at all and later that afternoon during a break I went up to her office to return her money out of my own pocket. I received the shock of all shocks. Apparently when Sally returned to her office, her boss had fired her, so she was not there. I don't know how she avoided my watchful eye when she made her exit but apparently she managed it.

She had tried to be a legal secretary but she was so unsure of herself that it prevented her from doing the good job that she was capable of doing because she was so nervous all of the time. Her boss knew that her expertise was being a receptionist and PBX operator and he knew of a friend that needed her abilities. He drove her over to meet this man and the man hired her on the spot. In the meantime, Sally knew of a legal secretary who was looking for work and gave her ex-boss the telephone number. He called her the next day for an interview and hired her immediately. So everyone was happy but ME!

I was still determined to get her money back to her as I knew she was not only supporting her two little boys, Jeff and Greg, but contributing a lot to her mom as well. At this point school had let out for the summer and her boys were leaving to spend the summer with their father.

The following Saturday, I found myself at the Villa Marina searching for her. I wasn't disappointed but the real luck was that she was there with her mother and some old family friends. I walked up to her, leaned over and taking her left hand in mine, placed her money in it and proceeded to tell her all about what had happened to me, in trying to get her money back to her. She thought that was funny and I was relieved to hear that everything had turned out for her. I told her that I was meeting my best buddy at the bar for a drink and asked if she might dance with me later. She liked that idea, and about an hour later we were out on the floor, dancing up a storm.

The dance floor was lit dimly by black light, which gave everything and everyone on the floor a very dark blue color. There was a mural of a seascape done with fluorescent paint on the back wall of the dancing area and it glowed. Strangely enough, so did white shirt collars and cuffs. In fact anything white would glow. Sally was wearing a very pale pink and fairly thin nylon dress and she looked very pretty in it. She happened to glance down only to find that she could see her bra and matching lace panties gleaming merrily right through her thin dress. She was horrified, as though she had just discovered she was stark naked and covered up as best as she could, while running off the dance floor. She really was embarrassed but at the same time thought it was hilariously funny. So did I.

I asked her if she could leave her mother and her mother's friends and come with me for awhile. That was no problem and said her farewells and we were off.

I was driving a red convertible Austin-Healy sports car and the top was down. Before we got in, I politely asked her if she'd like me to put the top up so her long hair wouldn't blow. Her answer made me fall in love with her all over again. "There isn't anything that can happen to my hair that a comb can't fix," as she tossed it at me. With that, I started my little car and we roared off to Laguna Beach, which is just down the coast from Newport. I had no idea that she didn't drink much alcohol and I ordered a couple of triples for her when we stopped at a bar. They didn't seem to affect her one way or another and we talked and laughed the night away, right up to the time the place closed at two in the morning.

Pacific Coast Highway, which had only two lanes back in 1961 was practically deserted at this late hour and it was a clear moonlit night. On the way back to Newport Beach something happened that was so odd, even spooky, that to this very day neither Sally nor I have ever figured it out. But there really is only one answer.

There is no doubt that I was driving too fast, 90 mph. My Austin-Healy was designed for speed and handling and I felt I was in complete control. Sally didn't seem to be uncomfortable in the passenger seat either when suddenly, my headlights picked up something about two hundred yards directly in front of us. It was a four-door gray sedan stalled broadside in the middle of the road. I could plainly see a thin, middle-aged man wearing glasses sitting on the driver's side and a plump, middle-aged woman, probably his wife, seated next to him in the passenger seat. As we bore down upon them I could see their faces which were frozen in terror. The gray sedan was taking up enough of both lanes that there was no way I could swerve around it at the speed we were going. There was nothing I could do but keep going and I didn't even think about putting on the brakes, which would probably have made the situation worse. If we were going to die, it might as well be a quick death. But we didn't die. We never even hit that other car because it just disappeared! Sally never said a word.

We continued on in silence, at a much slower speed, for about two minutes and finally I couldn't stand it anymore and asked Sally if she had seen anything. *Sally had seen exactly what I had seen and described the stricken sedan and its occupants right down to the man's glasses!* She told me she had thought, "Oh, I'm going to die," but she was so relaxed from all the booze that she decided not to fight it and let it happen. It didn't scare her a bit. When I mentioned it, she realized that she had already forgotten all about it and then realized that she had not died and that nothing had happened to either one of us. Today we both know that the Angels were working overtime that night, saving our lives for God's unknowable purpose. It just wasn't our time to leave this wonderful Earthplane and we both thank You, Father God for sending Your Angels to us.

Sally and I became a couple after that momentous first date. We had a swell summer together and finally it was time for her two boys to return home from visiting their dad and start back to school. Sally lived with her mother who took care of the boys while Sally was at work. Even though I loved her madly, I wasn't ready to commit myself again to being a family kind of guy. Do you notice a little selfishness here? I told myself that I was too restless to settle down and I liked to party too much to get married. Even though I really liked Sally's young boys, I figured my wild ways would eventually cause a lot of heartbreak for all of us and Sally must have sensed this, too. We slowly drifted apart but remained good friends. Humorous greeting cards were becoming a big fad then as they are today and I'd often receive one from Sally. Sometimes we would phone one another to share some good joke that was going around and we'd both laugh ourselves silly every time. We have always shared the same visual sense of humor. We'd both see the same pictures in our heads conjured up by some great joke and we would elaborate on the situation by seeing it from different points of view, making it even funnier. This has never changed in all the years we've known each other.

One Monday evening about four months after we'd stopped dating, she called me. She was babysitting for her brother's partner for a few hours and said she had a priceless joke for me. We laughed our heads off over it. I ended up telling her that I'd missed her and had never had as much fun with anyone else as I did with when we were together. Finally, I asked her if she would like to have a drink with me somewhere on Thursday evening. This was fine with her. I guess I was in the process of rethinking my views about being a family man and I was really looking forward to seeing her again. Fate was making other plans.

After our phone conversation that night, Sally found that her evening was far from over. Her babysitting was finished by 9:30 and when she got back home, her neighbor came running out and asked Sally to go with her and help look for her boyfriend who had left after some stupid argument. She wanted to go to him and make up. Sally graciously said O.K. but inside she wasn't happy about it.

They went to a little joint called The Anchor Cove where the boyfriend regularly hung out. He wasn't there but it seemed like a good idea to stick around awhile and wait to see if he would eventually turn up. He never did, but while they were waiting Sally realized that she'd seen the bartender before. He only did his bartending between jobs as a crewmember on chartered boats. This bartender didn't seem to like Sally very much as he was always short to the point of rudeness with her even though she could think of nothing she had ever done to receive this kind of treatment from him.

This particular evening, however, the two girls sat and chatted with this bartender right up to "last call" and this time the guy was civil to Sally for a change. While he was closing the bar he asked both girls if they would like to join him for breakfast at an all night coffee shop. Sally's lovelorn girlfriend declined because she hoped her boyfriend might have returned to her place by this time. But Sally, Samaritan that she is, felt sorry for the lonely bartender and since he had been so uncharacteristically pleasant to her all night, she accompanied him to the coffee shop. She just didn't think he should have to eat alone and come to think of it she was a little hungry herself.

I have a little trouble believing what happened next, but Sally assures me this is what occurred.

As they talked during their breakfast, the man mentioned that he had been hired to be the engineer on a huge yacht that was heading down to Acapulco, Mexico in about three weeks and would she like to accompany him? She jokingly replied, "Sure, if you give me your name," meaning, if he married her. He thought about that for a minute or so and then said, "I'd be delighted to give you my name." It was a strange proposal from a strange guy. Sally must have been testing him because she said she

159

would marry him and just like that they were engaged! And darned if they didn't actually get married on his 37th birthday, three weeks later, two days before leaving for Acapulco. Everyone who knew her was shocked, and why not? She was a "nice" girl and he had a dubious reputation. He had absolutely nothing to offer her. He was a huge man, 6'5" tall and had a 52-inch chest. She was 5'3" and weighed in at a mere 115 pounds. Sally had her reasons for this surprising move. She didn't like the merry-go-round of dating and spending most evenings out drinking in bars. She didn't really enjoy liquor at all. And she didn't like living with her mother, either. She thought that maybe this would be a good way out of her current rut.

Their marriage lasted for over eleven years and yes, there were some really nice times but he was a periodic alcoholic and went on binges. There were two good things that came out of this union and their names are Dean and Reid, two fantastic kids. Sally's marriage somewhat paralleled my marriage with Eve — the good times were super and the bad times were nightmares. I saw her around town from time to time for awhile, but finally there came a long period when I didn't see her at all.

Chapter Sixteen

SALLY

I was due to go back into the hospital for my second hip transplant on December 12th and it was now November. I was in my "party animal" stage and beginning to feel the need for a little stability, when out of the blue I got a telephone call from my old flame, Sally. I hadn't seen or spoken with her for almost seven years. She told me I was hard to track down and it had taken her three days to find me. She asked me if I remembered her. Remember her? And how! I honestly didn't believe it was really her, but I was just delighted, even it was some trick. After talking with her, I waited about ten minutes and called her back just to see if it was a joke and to find out if it was really, *really* her. And it *was* Sally. She said she would come to see me the very next day. She told me she remembered how happy I always seemed to be and said that she just wanted to see my smile again and I told her how badly I wanted to see her. What she really needed was a job of some sort . . . she said that she wasn't interested in any relationship but just wanted to concentrate on her work and the raising of her two youngest sons who were now six and nine years old. But she did want to see me smile, and that was encouraging.

Her oldest son, Jeff, was married and working and her nineteen year old, Greg, was an X-ray technician in the U.S. Air Force. Dean and Reid had been living with their father in Arizona for the past few months. She had missed Halloween with them and was about to miss Thanksgiving and Christmas, too. It was unbearably painful for her to be without them. She wanted a good job so she could support them. At that moment Arizona was the best place for them because her ex-husband's family lived there and she knew that her sons were being well taken care of and their father was good to them. But she needed a job to get some earning power so she could take care of them on her own. She was so happy when I told her that I could fix up something for her.

We met at 10:30 the next morning on a bus bench of all places. Sally never learned how to drive so a bus stop seemed like the logical place to hook up. About two seconds after she got into the car, we had sized each other up and come to the conclusion that neither of us had changed that much physically since last seeing each other. She was forty and I was forty-one. Even though it was only mid-morning, the first place I took her was a bar. Sadly, I really "needed" a drink. She told me she had entirely stopped drinking years ago. She had never smoked either. She just never enjoyed either of these vices.

All of a sudden I found myself saying, "I lost you twelve-and-a-half years ago and I never want you further away from me than this. I'm going to marry you." Sally blinked and asked, taken aback, "What on earth made you say that?" I couldn't put it into words but I just "knew" that I didn't want her away from me ever again. From that moment on we have never really been apart and we were married quietly a short time later. But that first night after seeing each other after so many years, we literally spent the entire day and all that night catching up on our lives and exchanging new jokes and funny stories. We laughed to the point of exhaustion and begged each other, no more . . . and then it would start all over again.

I didn't want her to know that I was an alcoholic and I on this day hadn't touched another drop, after the one drink I had that morning in the bar. We had literally stayed up all night and it was the longest I'd been away from a cocktail in years. By eight in the morning I wasn't feeling very well, in fact I started to get very sick to my stomach. Sally started to rush out for some stomach medicine at the local drug store to stop me from throwing up. I called out to her as she was leaving, "Pick up a pint of Bourbon while you're at it." I knew what I really needed . . . my own sweet poison . . . my medication . . . my crutch . . . my whiskey.

Sally did as I asked. When she returned, she dosed me with the patent stomach remedy, which immediately came right back up. Then I opened Dr. Booze's Remedy for the DTs and downed a couple of big slugs of it. Lo and behold, I stopped being sick. We were both completely bushed from staying up all night and fell asleep after my little cure.

Sally still didn't quite yet understand that I didn't have the flu, and when she woke up she went out again and came back with some cream of chicken soup. I hate cream of chicken soup and although I thanked her profusely, I couldn't drink it. Since we had forgotten to eat the night before, we thought it would be nice to go out for some breakfast. When I stopped on the way for another bottle of Bourbon, the light dawned on Sally what the real problem was, yet she didn't seem to mind, as I never acted drunk. The drinking was *my* problem. She infinitely understood and I was grateful later on that it hadn't kept her from marrying me.

Sally is a great student of metaphysics. The Science of Metaphysics deals with a number of spiritual questions and especially those words in the Bible that say, basically, *"that which ye sow, so shall ye reap."* Nowadays we say, "What goes around, comes around." It all boils down to the fact that you and only you are responsible for your actions on Earth, good or bad. You might not get any rewards or retribution on this plane, but at some time in your spiritual, eternal existence you will get exactly what you deserve based upon what you have done in this world. It is the law of cause and effect. Sally believes that God never sends bad things. God loves us and is *for* us, not against us. We bring on illness and accidents and bad situations by our thoughts, speech and actions. She knows that you have to be careful with your beliefs and she surrenders her days to God as best she can, and lets His will be done. God only wants good things for us and to aid us. God's Angels are His helpers and messengers.

You have heard the term "born again". That is when a person realizes he is a spiritual being as well as a material being and gets a new insight into what we *truly* are — a creation of God, in His image. We are mind, body and spirit just as He is.

You must remember to live in the present moment. We miss so much by living in the past or dwelling too much on the future. Sally also says that our words are very important and have great bearing on how we prosper, not just monetarily, but in physical health and fruitful relationships with others in our lives. She believes that saying positive affirmations can change fear into something wonderful and peaceful. She has taught me this and she is right — prayer and positive affirmations work if you'll just let go and let God do his work. He knows your every need! It's not easy to really change your thinking and the way you speak, and the first step is allowing God and His Angels into your heart.

We are born here on Earth for only two reasons: to learn and to help others to learn. We are here to learn how to be closer to our Creator, to learn to entrust Him with our cares and woes. Believe me, He can come up with some very creative solutions!

Sally has a very clear head. She enabled me to see that I was self-destructing over a huge guilt that I had concerning Eve and the children. She suggested that I weigh that situation on an imaginary scale and see who ended up with what. On the one side, Eve still had her children, her fame, her good looks and reputation, power, loving fans, great wealth and a career that was intact. I had what I carried out to the car with me when I left. My health was bad. I drank too much. I had no money and I couldn't even work at my profession because of my hip transplants. Sally told me, "Why on Earth are you feeling sorry for Eve? Eve had ended up with *everything* and you came out with *nothing*!" For Eve, life had continued on just as it had been before we were married. As for me, I didn't even have my businesses any more. I had given up the barbershops during my marriage and didn't get them back after the divorce. But as far as Sally was concerned, *the score was even*! The slate was clean. Don't dwell on it. Let it go. The children were the ones who really got hurt. They were the true victims.

The one thing I really needed to do was forgive myself. It can be easy to forgive others, but forgiving yourself can be mighty tough. It didn't happen overnight, but with Sally's help my thinking clarified and as time went by I became a better person. There is a saying, "Be patient with me, God isn't finished with me, yet." I think that applies to all of us, and very much to me. At that time God had barely started on me.

Chapter Seventeen

MEDICAL PROBLEMS

When it was time for my operations, Sally stayed with me and the only time she left my side was to go home to eat and get a few hours of sleep. No one could ask for a better caretaker and watchdog than Sally if they happen to be in the clutches of Doctors and their allies, The Hospital Staff.

Before the operation she had contacted the Church of Religious Science, Ministry of Prayer, in Los Angeles, California and asked them to pray for me and they did. They prayed for thirty days, before, during, and after the operation and I got my little miracle. The cancerous tumor in my leg was removed safely without breaking and I did not lose my leg. And here is something interesting. This type of operation is supposed to take three to four hours but mine was finished in just one hour and forty-five minutes! It was unheard of at that time and my doctors were pretty amazed. Here is something else I consider a medical miracle. My hip transplants were only supposed to last eight to ten years at the most before needing to be redone. Mine are still with me after more than twenty-five years and X-rays show that they look brand new. How about that!

So two years after the operations I was doing much better physically but I was still drinking heavily. I knew in my heart that this demon had to go. The spirit was willing but the flesh was weak. I had moved close to my family and entered into all the family activities. Constant drinking was *not* their way of life. I was blessed with a large clan, not just my brothers and sister, but also a multitude of aunts and uncles, cousins, nephews and nieces. We all love each other unconditionally. We don't judge each other. When one of us is in need, the family is there for them. We also leave each other alone if that happens to be what will help. If one or more of us misses a family gathering, his or her absence will be noted, but no one will talk about them behind their backs. I love them dearly and I wanted to be like them — sober. I just didn't know how to go about it. Every time I tried to stop I got so sick. Because of my constant failures to get off the sauce I was not always my usual cheerful self. Then I got another miracle.

My parents are buried in a cemetery that is located behind the house in which we were living at the time. There is a stairway in back of the house that leads up to their gravesite. One day, Sally went up those stairs, walked over to my parents' plots and, even though she had never met them said, "Dad and Mom, I am losing the battle with Glenn's love affair with the bottle. I promise you, no matter what happens that I will never leave him, not even if he tries to kill me. But please, just give me a sign and I will carry the ball, but at this point I really don't know what to do." She thanked them and told them she would be waiting for the sign. Well, three days later the booze really turned on me. I couldn't drink a drop of the stuff without throwing up. But I was at a point in my life where I couldn't even get out of bed in the morning without my glass full of Bourbon with very little water (no ice). How's that for a catch-22? I really *needed* liquor to get through the day but I could no longer drink it. I knew the time had come for me to act. Life was no longer fun. In fact it was pure misery. I just lay in bed for the next four days watching one particular movie channel on TV. One of the station's sponsors was a hospital for alcoholics.

As Sally left for work on the fourth morning, I asked her to make a call to that hospital and she did. That very night after Sally came home from work I went into rehabilitation. It took only two weeks to change the rest of my life, and I haven't touched a drop of liquor in any form for over twenty-three years! Of course the Ministry of Prayer was called and asked to pray for me and Sally sent out prayers every day. So, again I thank You, Father God. Thank you for my new life and for my successful operations. Thank You! Praise You! I love you.

After I sobered up, I was blessed to retain my happy-go-lucky attitude and my big smile, but I found an unpleasant surprise awaiting me. About two months after my release from rehab, Sally noticed that I had a constant, nagging little cough and that I had lost about twenty pounds in little more than two weeks. She said it looked as though my head was sitting atop a broom handle. I was also running a low fever and had no energy. I went to the doctor for a checkup and was immediately hospitalized. After a session with my old friend, the X-ray machine the doctors discovered that I was suffering from moderately advanced tuberculosis. What's next, God? Are you testing me? Surprisingly, after only three days in the hospital I was sent home as if I had a common cold. I was told to stay in bed and I'd be up and around in about a month. How about four-and-a-half months on my back only getting up to go to the bathroom. I was in total agony. All I did was sleep, sweat pools of water at night (these are known as night sweats) and I could eat only fresh food prepared from scratch.

I was absolutely helpless and Sally had to do everything for me. No one could assist her, as I was extremely contagious. She had to wear a mask at all times in the house and disinfect everything around me every day. She was my personal Mother Teresa during this trying time. She had to prepare three full meals every day. I was so hungry! I ate enough bananas to satisfy an entire troop of monkeys because I needed the potassium that bananas supply. I needed the potassium because I was losing so much water during my night sweats. Sally knows that only God could have gotten her through this miserable period.

Aside from the almost full time care she was giving me, she had her regular job to do, too. She put in extra hours at work to build up time off so she could take me to my doctor appointments. I was not getting well and the doctors eventually found that I was allergic to the medication I had been taking for a month. Then another month went by with no medication at all and I was not improving in the slightest. Then I had another miracle. A new TB medicine was discovered prescribed for me and I was healed within a short time. Thank you once more, Father God! And thank you,

Ministry of Prayer for all your prayers during this lengthy sickness.

Chapter Eighteen

MY FIRST NEAR-DEATH EXPERIENCE

Our house had lots of windows and during my illness all the shades were drawn to make it easier for me to sleep during the day. One happy morning when I finally felt my strength begin to return, I got up and opened the shades. I found that it had snowed that day and cars were having a hard time getting up the hill on which we lived. It was comical. I was like a little kid, going from window to window, watching these cars struggling up our hill. It was so exciting to see life again! For the next three days I got up and opened the window shades and looked out with pleasure at the trees and the cars and people going by. But the fourth day was different. I felt very tired and didn't get up at all. By mid-afternoon I felt overpoweringly sleepy, but I couldn't get to sleep. Sally was at work so I was alone. You must remember that I had been *getting better* after my long sickness, and that's what makes what happened next so weird.

My spirit left my body. All of a sudden I was *five feet above my bed looking down at myself.* At first I didn't comprehend what I was seeing. I looked and stared and wondered who was in the bed and then the realization hit that it was *myself* and I looked so old and thin. I was down to 123 pounds from the tuberculosis — just skin and bones. After getting used to the strange phenomenon of being outside my body, I lost interest in myself and drifted into the living room and then went right up through the roof of the house. I paused and gazed around, happy and content to be outside and then I shot up and up and up until I could no longer even see Earth. I found myself in pitch-blackness and I had the feeling that I was in a very dark tunnel. I was moving at tremendous speed. There was a sense of being surrounded by many other souls and I could hear a deep humming vibration that was comforting rather than eerie. Then I began to hear singing — joyous, beautiful singing. I can't, I am sorry to say, describe this music. All I can say is that I have never heard anything like it on Earth.

I was rushing toward that bright light that has been described by so many others that have had their own near-death experiences. When I saw this light, which was a blinding bright but did not hurt my eyes, I was awed and overwhelmed with a feeling of vast, unconditional love and peace that was beyond comprehension. I felt a tremendous joy and all I

could think of was that I was going home . . .
going *home*! As I emerged from the tunnel into
the light, I saw a shining male spirit in the midst
of a small plain of upturned faces. These faces
had no bodies. Suddenly I became one of those
faces.

The beautiful spiritual entity was clothed in
a white robe and was moving amongst all the
upturned faces. I felt it was Jesus. I thought this
because there was a light shining from His face
that was so bright that no matter how hard I
looked, I couldn't make out His features. Every
now and then He would extend His arm and
hold his hand above one of the heads. He
would sometimes pick up one of the faces,
which would then just disappear, from His
hand. The longing to be chosen, like a head of
cauliflower, was so intense, so desired, that
there are no words to explain it. My soul's every
atom wanted to be in this Being's hand and
strained towards it. Some faces He passed by.
Then He came to me and held His hand for a
long time over my head. But He didn't pick me
and I was devastated. The next thing I knew, I
was back in my body on Earth feeling heavy and
horrible after being so happy and free. I, who
loved life beyond words and who adored my
Sally, wanted only one thing — to go back
where I had just been.

When Sally walked up the hill that afternoon on her way home from work, she saw that the shades had not been pulled back and she thought, "Oh dear God, please don't let him be dead!" She felt something was terribly wrong and started running towards the house. She burst through the door expecting the worst. She found me sleeping peacefully. Incredibly relieved, she thanked God above that her worst fears were unrealized.

I finally got well but I didn't tell Sally about my experience. If I had tried to talk about it I would have started crying and I didn't want to do that in front of her. I had never heard of anyone coming back after dying, except maybe Lazarus in the Bible, and actually, I didn't know that I'd died. I only knew that I'd had that most humbling, unimaginable experience.

Chapter Nineteen

LESSONS

About five months later, after I had finished washing Sally's hair, she said, "Glenn, you are so good to me. You're such a wonderful person." I managed to say, "I'll never be good enough." She bridled at that and asked me to repeat what I'd just said, so I repeated it. She responded, "Why would you say anything like that? You're the nicest person I've ever know in my whole life." For the first time I felt able to tell her what happened to me while I was sick. She wasn't all that surprised, as she knew about near-death experiences from books she had read in the 1960's. I told her that I felt that I hadn't been good enough to be taken into Jesus' hand. She responded to this by saying, "Glenn, that's just not true. You weren't taken because it just wasn't "your time" yet. God has a plan for you and you must be patient until you complete whatever He needs you to do." She explained that God assigns some people really big tasks. Others might be chosen for a lot of little jobs that seem small to us but are very *big* to Him. A very few are asked by God to do huge, monumental things. She said it doesn't matter what our assignment is, but it does matter how we live our lives. We must do the best we can until God takes us in His good time. She reminded me that God is so vast and complex that a person could spend a lifetime studying Him and not even scratch the surface of how wonderful He is.

She continued on about the millions of souls out there that are spiritually bankrupt, some of which are working so frantically for money and power that, even after they have attained everything they could possibly want, feel empty inside. These people think that acquisition is all there is to life. Some of them turn to drugs, alcohol or both - never learning that only God can fill the empty places in their souls with a glory that transcends human understanding.

Then she went on about the poor and unloved on this Earth that have just plain given up. They are simply unaware of how special they are in God's eyes and that He has a plan for every single soul in the universe. We live in a world where a smile at the right time can change a person's mind about committing suicide. Mankind is so little and thinks it's so great, but even so, God loves us dearly. All we have to do is turn to Him, not just once in awhile, but every day and let Him know how grateful for what He has given us — just being alive is such a privilege.

It helped me to listen to her. Of course, my experience on the other side of that tunnel had changed me. When I was able to return to my normal life, I found that I couldn't stand to be around violence or people arguing. I had a need to avoid all negativity. I was more appreciative of every little thing, every precious moment of life, and I wanted the whole world to feel the same way I did. The doctors had healed my TB, but God had healed my spirit. After I was well, I was at peace with myself and with my world.

Since that time I have said long prayers of thankfulness to God every morning and every evening. I pray not only for my family, friends, and loved ones, but also for the whole world. I will never stop doing this. So much has taken place in my life to make it full and happy. Eventually, Sally was able to have her sons, Dean and Reid returned to her and I was able to share in the fulfilling experience of raising them to adulthood. I can say with a full heart that I feel that I had a big share in helping them become the wonderful adults they are today.

There have been a few sad times since my illness. My brothers, Jay and Dutch died several years apart. If I hadn't known what glory was awaiting them, I would have been devastated, but knowing what was on "the other side" helped me immeasurably when they passed on.

Chapter Twenty

GOOD THINGS TO KNOW

Here are the ways that Sally and I cope with life. We face unpleasantness head-on. We do what we can to solve each situation right away. If there is a problem that seems insoluble, which has happened only a few times, we take this problem straight to God and seek His guidance. It's like magic. Everything just falls right into place.

We take care of business as it comes up. We pay our bills on time and thank our Precious Lord that He has provided the money to do so. We are responsible adults and we work as a team, leaning on each other's strengths and filling in for each other's weaknesses. We know that the past cannot hurt us because we won't allow it to. We take nothing for granted especially not each other.

We are very appreciative of each other and try to be kind, considerate, thoughtful, caring and loving. You simply cannot beat that combination. We would each rather die than do something hurtful to one another. We are polite, never omitting a "please" or "thank you" when it is called for. We compliment each other when we look nice or do a good job at something. Love is behavior. And here is something very important. We are not in competition about anything. We share what we learn and we share our day when we each get home. In short, we enjoy almost everything about each other. We are devoted. We don't analyze every thought as to why we are doing something for the other or think what we are going to get out of it when we go out of our way to do something special for each other. We allow our lives to unfold in Divine order and because of that we don't have many waves of contention. We try and talk about potential problems before they become real problems. We stay very close to God in our hearts and it's usually smooth sailing. We act the way we do toward each other because we *want* to, not because we're *expected* to. Being the way we are toward each other, combined with our closeness to God makes for a very nice life. It also helps to be organized to avoid confusion. Believe me, this makes life a *lot* easier.

Sally and I have survived some pretty rough times including illnesses not even mentioned in this book, but no matter how horrible it's gotten, for some reason we've always been able to find the humor in every adversity. We can laugh and laugh to the point where people think we're crazy. That's just the way we are. She is my Earth Angel and I am hers and we both know it. It will always be like this, until God asks us to come home.

You know, I wish everybody could see the funny side of life the way we do. You have to concentrate on the wonders of life and not just all the awful things that can crop up from time to time. We try and make it a nicer world for everyone whom we might meet. People don't want to hear sad songs. They want to see joyful faces and ready smiles and welcoming arms. There's nothing wrong with talking about things that have happened to you that are not pleasant, but try to put a positive twist at the end your story. When you put out positive words, they come back to you. Really! Just making a little change in the way you answer your telephone can make a difference. By putting warmth into your greeting, a cheery hello, will make the person on the other end feel so welcomed.

***

After looking back on my life I've come to these conclusions. I've been a good son. I honored my mother and father. I always tried to make my family proud of me and even when I didn't succeed I never stopped trying. I was a better than average student in school. When I was in the Korean War, I helped to save many, many young men's lives by being in the Medical

Corps. I have been a good friend. I have been a good husband. I have been a good brother. I have raised two wonderful sons and I have shown them my love and taught them love. I have traveled most everywhere, enough to see everything in this world I ever wanted to see. I've seen nothing I need to see again. I have loved and been loved. I like the direction my life is going.

I know that I have had a great ride so far and being here has been a ball no matter what! If I didn't make it through the next 24 hours, so be it. I have had my life and it has been wonderful. I know that as long as the spirit is in the body there will *always* be room for improvement. But that is why we are here, to learn, experience and to grow spiritually by getting close to God. Consider all your problems, be they little or big. God has the answer to everything and He loves you more than you can ever imagine. He will always take care of you.

Think about this. So many of us say we love God, but how many of us *allow God to love us back!* Think about what Jesus said in the Bible. *"I have come to give you life and that life more abundantly."* Does it say, "I have come to make you suffer?" No! Doesn't "abundantly" mean "lots of"? I think it means having a wonderful family, plenty of money for all your needs, wonderful friends and being surrounded by love and joy . . . all good things!

Chapter Twenty-One

DEATH AND THE CELESTIAL KINGDOM

Let me continue from where I left off in Chapter One. You might remember that I had suffered a major heart attack and was lying in my hospital bed, alone and scared witless. It was a long night, I couldn't sleep and I was doing a little review of my life to pass the time.

The next day was Sunday. Our son Reid and his girlfriend Dana came to see me. I guess I wasn't very hospitable to them and they left quickly to go home and pick up Sally and bring her back to the hospital. I still wasn't being nice to Sally, either, and when she came into my room I told her that I didn't want to see the kids again. Well, she told me in no uncertain terms that they were scared to death about my condition and they wanted to come back in and say goodbye and that I was going to be decent to them for at least a half a minute. Sally went out and Reid and Dana came back in. This time I behaved myself and they were able to give a much more positive report to Sally when they returned to her. Both kids felt much better as I seemed more like myself.

On Monday morning Sally, having no idea how I was going to treat her and determined not to upset me if at all possible, peeked at me from around the doorway and there I was back to my normal, buoyant self. I was so happy to see her. I didn't remember being mean to her. She knew that and didn't bring it up. She sat down close to me and held my arm, there was no place she could hold my hand because of wires that were connected to every finger on both hands. She took one look at me and I took one look at her and we looked at where we were and we looked at all the medical stuff around us and we got the giggles. I said to her, "What in the world did I do to deserve this?" We started to laugh all over again. It all seemed absurd. Everything had been wonderful in our world and then, bingo — I almost died! What was this all about? Off and on, all through the day, Sally did hands on Reiki, sending healing energy through my body. When the nurses and doctors came to check on me, she would slip out to the chapel in the hospital and pray. The nurse allowed her to stay until about ten when our wonderful John came and took her home.

I am so sorry that I was so unpleasant to my loved ones. I really have no recollection, even today, about being mean spirited. Sally told me all about it much later, after I was out of the woods.

On Wednesday morning they placed a catheter through my groin and ran it up to my heart to see how much damage had been done. But just as it touched my heart I suffered a coughing spell, which caused the catheter to bruise the heart. After the doctor and medical staff calmed down, they did what they needed to do and got done what they needed done. They told me I had to hold my legs stiff and not bend them for twelve hours. They actually strapped them down and Sally had to sit there for every one of those hours and watch to make sure I didn't move those legs. This was tough going because I could easily bend my knees.

In the middle of the night I was moved from Intensive Care to a wardroom. But around 7am, my heart started to beat very irregularly from the bruising it had taken the day before. It took five hours to stabilize. I never felt dizzy or had any pain. This puzzled the doctors. It happened a few more times during that day and it carried over to the next day.

I was scheduled to go home on a Friday. My lady doctor came in and said, "I just don't feel quite right about letting you go home today. You have become my favorite patient and I don't want anything to happen to you." (As you read this chapter you will see why I'm glad she felt that way.) On Saturday about 1:30pm, a nurse came in and gave me a pill and said, "This ought to do the trick." Both Sally and I had a strange feeling about this pill, but neither of us spoke up. We didn't trust that still, small voice saying, "Don't take this pill." . . . big mistake!

A couple of hours later, I got up to use the bathroom and as I got back into bed I and told Sally that I had felt very dizzy for a second while I was in the john. Sally immediately called the nurse and she ran in but could find nothing wrong with me, and we dismissed the dizziness as a fluke.

Sally and I were looking forward to watching "Dave" on HBO, which was to start at six PM. The movie had been on for only a few minutes when I felt a little dizzy and a bit nauseated and very quietly and calmly, said "Honey . . . " Sally immediately turned her head to respond to me and I was dead. *That fast!* My eyes were wide open and my face was pulled back as if a hundred-G forces were peeling my lips back. Sally thought I was making a funny face and she said, "Oh, Glenn that's not funny. . . . *Stop it!*" She thought I was still breathing because there were tiny puffs of air escaping from my mouth. She kept asking me to stop trying to be funny. I didn't move and it took her about 45 seconds to realize that something was terribly wrong.

She glanced down on the bed but couldn't find the button that called the nurse. She didn't know that the nurses had a display of my monitors at their station. When Sally couldn't find the nurse signal, she quickly tried to give me mouth to mouth resuscitation, but my mouth was so rigid that she couldn't get any air into me. Finally she panicked and ran to the hallway yelling, "Code 3 . . . Code 3 . . . or Code Blue. *Code SOMETHING!*" She knew that one of those meant *emergency!* (Naturally, we laughed about this later) The nurses were running towards her as fast as they could, yelling back to her that they saw it on their monitor. Three women came running out of their loved one's hospital rooms where they were visiting and rushed to hold Sally. Later, my wife said it was just like in the movies with the crash cart and the loudspeaker going and all the doctor's running out of the elevators to my room. The concerned nurses were running back and forth and finally they told Sally that they had saved me.

At one point she said she felt what is known as the "widow's wail", a force so primal that there is nothing you can do about it. It starts at the bottom of your feet and goes up your body.

Fortunately, this one stopped in her chest because she got good news — I was back. But if it had gone the other way, she says she would have made an absolutely inhuman sound.

The doctors had no way of knowing that I was allergic to that particular medication. The drug was Quinidine. It's a commonly used drug for heart patients. Unfortunately, in my case it killed me.

Here's how it felt for me to die. Remember, this all happened very quickly. I felt my toes and feet go numb and then the numbness continued up my legs, to my stomach and then to my chest. When the numbness got to my chest I stopped breathing. The numbness continued to go up my neck and throat and then my eyes failed and I could see nothing. The last sense to go was my hearing. I heard my last breath leave my body. Then I felt three little jerks . . . At my knees, my stomach and my chest and then I felt like a little door was opening in the back top part of my head and I felt as if my *whole being* went through that little door.

I found myself at the top of the ceiling in my hospital room. I saw Sally jump up and shake me and I saw her trying to give me CPR. I watched her run out of the room and heard her yelling for help. I saw the crash cart coming, rolling down the hallway. I saw the doctors and the nurses take their place around my bed, frantically trying to bring me back to life. At first I couldn't see who the person on the bed was and I was wondering what they were doing to that poor person, when one of the nurses moved and I saw that it was me.

Then I went into a brief darkness, but I was not alone. There was a being with me. I heard him say, "Glenn, we must leave now." I answered him by saying, "No, I can't leave. It would be much too horrible for Sally."

Nevertheless, I found myself looking down on the top of the hospital and felt myself rising higher and higher until I was watching the world grow smaller and smaller until it no longer was there. I felt myself speeding through the void until I was in a totally dark place looking down on all creation. I saw the stars and planets of the universe far below me. Then, even those disappeared.

I could hear deep, heavy vibrations going from one end of Creation to the other. After awhile, these vibrations rose in pitch until they became music, the most beautiful music I have ever heard or ever will hear, at least while I live on Earth. Now I was in total darkness and an indescribable feeling of warm, overwhelming love enveloped my entire being. I will never forget that feeling of love — and belonging. I felt a total oneness with all things.

My traveling companion and I just drifted for a long time in this darkness. I never saw his face, but I could feel his presence and his love and compassion for me. Then as we drifted, still in darkness, I saw way off in the distance a white spot. I couldn't tell if we were going toward it or if it was coming to us, but it grew larger and larger and eventually we were in front of it. It looked like a giant white tunnel, as best as I can describe it. The next thing I knew we were inside of it going up. It was like being inside a fluffy cloud. I could see the walls but nothing else. We drifted up and up until I could see this very bright light at the end of the tunnel. My companion turned to me and said, "Our journey is coming to an end soon and I want you to know that I love you and enjoyed being with you."

I don't know who that wonderful entity was. Maybe he was my Guardian Angel or my spirit guide. I knew he had been with me my entire life, and I felt great sadness that we were parting. We reached the end of the tunnel and he said "Behold."

I have never in my life seen anything as beautiful as what lay before me. The colors were literally out of this world. Never had I even imagined anything like it. There is no way to describe it. We on Earth are born with only five physical senses but in Heaven there must be more and I felt then that I had been given an extra one to be able to experience the unworldly beauty of this place. It was as if I'd only been able to see in black and white for my whole life and was experiencing color for the first time. Those colors were so intense that if I said they were blue, green, silver or gold you could not grasp how deep and brilliant these colors actually looked to me. I wish I had some way to convey to you what I was seeing, but it can't be done.

We stood by the tunnel entrance for awhile and I looked out over a large, beautiful city that seemed to be part of a limitless Kingdom. I saw tall eight-sided buildings jutting skyward like huge crystals. They were emerald green and pointed on top. There were many people, or entities most of whom seemed to be doing something, going about their business, but I had no idea what they were doing, and still don't. The city was large, stretching as far as the eye could see, and the colors I saw were silver, gold, green, white and blue.

I was then met by two new entities that told me they were my escorts. I asked to go into this Kingdom, but was not allowed to.   They escorted me over the city so I could see it but they did not take me down into it.

The buildings were, as I said, tall, eight-sided, and all were pointed on top. They were emerald green and almost transparent and shaped like giant crystals. The buildings glistened as if they were made of ice. The passageways were gold and silver and they shone as if they might be visible from a thousand miles away. Yet I saw no sun. The sky and city — this whole kingdom — seemed to generate its own illumination. Going back to the colors I mentioned before, they really are unexplainable. The closest description I can give is that if you took all the colors we have here on Earth and magnified them a thousand times, you would still not match the colors there. They are that brilliant.

Everything I saw on my escorted tour was breathtakingly gorgeous. It seemed that everything had its own little halo around it. It was a strangely wonderful sensation traveling with my celestial escorts over the Kingdom of Heaven. I felt as if I had no weight, like a leaf in the wind. If I wanted to be somewhere, I would just wish it and I was there.

I was taken away from the city at a very high rate of speed. All I could see below me was a blurry, reddish kaleidoscope of color. At one point, we stopped and went down to about 200 feet above the surface and drifted slowly over the Kingdom. Once again, it was an outstanding sight to see. I spotted many things that resembled places we have here on Earth. I could see green, rolling hills and small oceans with white, sandy beaches and palm trees and high mountains with spectacular waterfalls cascading thousands of feet into a bright blue lagoon. The lagoon was surrounded by beautiful flowers of all colors... red, blue, lavender, and colors I have never seen before, perhaps only visible with that extra sense I had been given. I saw beings laughing and swimming in the lagoon. As we drifted slowly over, I thought it was an absolute island paradise, only more so if that makes any sense.

We continued to drift above the green, rolling hills. I saw what looked like Indians on horseback chasing a herd of buffalo. They didn't appear to be trying to hunt or hurt the buffalo; they were just chasing them. As we got closer, I could see that these animals were different than the buffaloes that I have seen on Earth; these were all white.

We drifted on and on. I could see children happily running and flying their brightly colored kites. I could see their pet dogs playing with them. They all looked happy as could be. As we continued our journey, I could see animals - elk, deer, bears, and cougars, even rabbits that hopped along with the rest. They all seemed to get along well with each other. They traveled in a group, side-by-side.

Traveling further, I could see large mansions with neatly trimmed hedges and beautiful, green grass, surrounded by white fences. I could see pretty little cottages along the cliffs above the ocean. I spotted large farmhouses with white fences and horses and cattle everywhere.

We passed over a mountain range and across an area that resembled a desert. I could see camels with riders. I could see great herds of sheep moving slowly across the desert to a cool, shady, beautiful oasis. As we got closer, I could see the sheep and sheepdogs lying in the shade resting, and among them were the lions of the desert laying among them enjoying the cool shade and resting side-by-side with the sheep. It was just like the Bible and the Garden of Eden.

I then began to realize that what I was being shown was the way life on Earth could be and I felt very sad and I wanted to cry. It was so beautiful and so peaceful.

We then began to drift back toward the city where I was escorted to a place that was made of marble. I found myself standing in front of a building with tall marble columns. There were four, maybe six, columns, which were very tall. I looked into a room with nothing in it but a large pedestal, also fashioned from marble, right in the center. The entities led me to the front of the pedestal and said, "You will go no closer than this." Then they left me standing there in front of the pedestal. One went off to my right as the other went off to my left and I was alone.

Suddenly a bright, bright light from above streamed down upon the pedestal. This was the brightest light I have ever seen. It was white, and so bright that if I were to see it on earth, I'm sure it would blind me. I stood in front of the light for a long time. The light seemed to penetrate my body. Only Good came out of that light, intense good. I felt love and such overwhelming love, that it enfolded my soul. I felt compassion, great compassion for everyone and everything. Above all, I felt truth in all things. I felt that everything in existence was sacred. Humbly, I knew this light *was* the face of God.

Like a fast-forward movie, I saw visions of newborn babies and mothers holding and loving their children, of old men and old women, of puppies with love in their hearts for their masters, of newlyweds being married. There were sunrises and sunsets, oceans
And mountains and everything that is good.

The light entirely surrounded my whole being and I felt that I was engulfed in everything ever created. I felt I was a part of it. I felt as if I had just come home from a long journey and was being met by all my loved ones. I felt important, as if I had held a very important position in this Kingdom and was being welcomed home as a hero.

Something was coming to me from the light — thousands of messages filling me with knowledge. The messages were teaching me that the people on Earth were all chosen by God to go there and help Him with His creation. That we were all Gods and all co-creators with God to create His paradise on Earth and that He has given us the power and the knowledge to create whatever we choose. These messages told me that we can create a Heaven or a Hell here on our planet and that whatever we choose to do is up to us. Most importantly, whatever comes from God, it is good. He wouldn't think of creating anything that wasn't good.

As I stood before the light, I found I could just think of a question in my head and the answer was there immediately. About religions? All paths that lead to God are good. Diseases? A thing of our own making. Sickness? What we eat, drink and think abuses our bodies. I learned that our thoughts can be as destructive to the human body as any diseases. Wars? A thing of our own making brought on by greed, envy, jealousy and hate. About accidental deaths? There are no accidents. It was explained that when we come to this earth, we are all given an equal amount of time to be here. In many cases, people die before there given time span is over and must come back to finish that time here. If a four-year-old child dies or is killed, it only means that it had a soul that died four years before its last life allotment was up. Yes, there is reincarnation.

Most importantly, I was told the three major laws of the universe and beyond. Number one: Love. Love everything and everybody. What you give you will receive. Number two: Compassion. Have compassion for everyone and everything. Number three: Truth. All the opposites of truth are bad — lies, deceit, cheating and so forth. If we live everyday in the light of truth, love and compassion, we will be following all the Commandments. I was told that Angels are God's messengers and are with everyone and are everywhere. It went on and on. So many questions and answers bombarded my mind that I couldn't possibly remember them all. In fact I'm sure there are many things I don't recall now because apparently, when we leave the celestial dimension to come back to earth, there are selective blockages imposed so we *can't* remember the entire experience

I stood there facing the pedestal and its light until the beam slowly faded and disappeared. It left me filled with love. More love than I have ever felt before. More compassion than I has ever known. It left me feeling that I was home at last.

The two entities that had escorted me to this wonderful place returned. One was speaking in a soft voice and I heard him whisper, "Then we must hurry." They both seemed very agitated. I asked them, "What is happening? What's wrong"? They explained that it wasn't my time to be here yet and that I must return to my body. I screamed, "No, No, Please — No!"

But, like it or not, back I went, shooting through the tunnel that had brought me to the Kingdom, this time in reverse — back to earth, then back into the hospital. The last thing I remember is following my earthly body, (which was in a bed being pushed from the wardroom), back down the hall to the intensive care unit. Then I was back in it, gasping for air and choking and vomiting.

I heard the nurse's voice telling me to stop fighting . . . to let the machine breath for me. I finally got the hang of it and then realized I was on a life support system to keep my heart beating and my lungs breathing. Let me tell you . . . if you had a billion dollars, you would give every penny of it in order to take that first wonderful breath of life. You can take my heartfelt word on this.

Eventually I settled down and the nurses started to clean me up. I was a total mess. When you die everything inside your intestines, stomach and bladder leaves you. It's gross . . . not a pretty picture.

Back amongst the living, I apologized to the nurses for making their job so difficult. They completely understood and told me they were glad to do it. Then these marvelous nurses welcomed me back to the world.

Sally was allowed to see me an hour later. She thought she was going to find me all pale and listless and weak and was flabbergasted to see me sitting up in bed, with pillows all plumped up behind me, smiling away . . . all pink and rosy and shiny. She kept exclaiming to the nurses that I just seemed to glow. I looked so healthy and she just couldn't believe her eyes. She couldn't get over seeing me this way after what I had just gone through. She did not know that I had actually died. Because of the puffing of air from my mouth, she thought I *was* dying and couldn't get air. It wasn't until the next day that she was told that I really had died. God is merciful.

The day after my death I awakened at seven in the morning. The curtains were open in my hospital room and the sun was shining and I looked out at the trees and the flowers and the big beautiful blue sky and everything that I could see seemed to have a light around it. Everything was so beautiful and I started to cry and cry and cry. It took me a quite awhile to stop these tears of happiness. I was so very glad to be alive.

I have to admit, no matter how beautiful my near-death experience was this time, I was really glad to be back in this wonderful/terrifying world and for about four days I was afraid to go to sleep. I didn't want to miss anything on this Earth. Life is so very precious. To see . . . to touch . . . to feel . . . to hear . . . to smell . . . to taste . . . how wonderful it all is!

So, here I was back at the hospital, back in my body, back in the intensive care ward. I felt okay, just very weak. The IV tubes, the wires attached to me, and the catheter in my bladder, were all very irritating. The nurses were checking on me about every 15 minutes, They were taking my temperature, pulse, respiration, and my fluid intake and output. They gave me so much attention that I don't think I could have died if I'd wanted to.

Later in the morning, I told one of the nurses about my near-death experience. She listened intently, hanging on every word. She didn't ask me any questions; she just heard me out and then left the room. When she left, I thought to myself, "Oh man, why did I say anything to her." The next thing I expected to see was a straight jacket and a trip to the psycho ward.

A half an hour later, the nurse returned. There were a lot of people with her. One lady had a chart and was taking notes. They asked me to repeat what I had told the nurse about my near-death experience and I did. I told them all that I could remember and then they asked me a lot of questions like, "When you were up there, looking down on us, can you remember where we were around your bed?" I answered every question and they kept looking around at each other. They never told me if I had answered correctly. They asked me so many questions, I can't remember them all now but I answered each one the best I could.

I didn't think they believed a word of my story. So as they were leaving the room, I said "If you need proof of my journey, have someone take a look on the top of the cabinet in the ward room and you will find a green Wrigley's chewing gum wrapper." This cabinet was where they had stored my clothes. It was a very heavy, tall cabinet that went almost up to the ceiling, so there is no way that I could have seen that wrapper while I was in bed or when I got up to go to the bathroom. They just smiled and thanked me and left as they entered, in a tight little group.

There was something I couldn't figure out — why would I die and then be sent back. I figured that I must have a job to do for God. But what was it? I didn't understand.

As for the hospital, the big day finally arrived, Tuesday, November 22, 1994. (It was also my first grandson Jackie's birthday.) The doctors came in, examined me, stood around my bed, and we talked and they gave me the good news that I could leave the hospital within the hour. They loaded me up with procedures for exercise, told me I had to do a lot of walking, and I had to stay on a diet they had for me. I couldn't wait to get out of there.

Sally was there with me. I got my clothes on and stood around for awhile. Then the doctor finally came in and said I could leave. We got into the elevator, went down to the first floor and we were just about out the door when a young lady came running up asking if I was Mr.

Maxwell. I answered affirmatively. She wanted to know if I was going home. Again I answered yes. She congratulated me and handed me an envelope, to which I didn't pay too much attention. After I got into the car, I checked the envelope to see what was in it. There was no note, nothing at all except one thing — the green Wrigley's chewing gum wrapper I'd seen when I was out of my body!

When I saw the gum wrapper I started laughing. Sally wanted to know what was so funny and I told her that I'd fill her in just as soon as we got home. Then I realized that I still had not told *her* of my near-death experience and she was the person I most wanted to know about it. When I did, Sally, who has no doubts whatever about an afterlife, accepted it without question.

Back at home, I felt good, and stuck to my new diet, basically just trying to get well again and become as strong as I was before my heart attack. I walked twice a day, once in the morning and again in the evening. At this point in my life, I became extremely spiritual. Who wouldn't? I became very sensitive to people's feelings. I became very compassionate, especially toward homeless people. This is the only time in my life I wished I had millions of dollars, so I could go out and give them away.

But I didn't have a million bucks and had to content myself with doing the best I could in my own simple way. As I took my evening walks, I found myself appreciating everything I passed. If I saw a flower, I would stop and enjoy the true beauty of its petals, its aroma. If I saw a bug on the pavement, I walked around it instead of stepping on it. Every blade of grass became precious. So did the trees, especially the trees. Where we live there are lots of trees and flowers. I can spend hours upon hours just walking through the foliage enjoying the beauty of the day.

After I got home from the hospital, I had a lot of quiet time. A time to think. A time to feel guilty for the things I had done wrong in my life. After being taken there, I believed in Heaven and being sent back. I sometimes wondered if being sent back was some kind of punishment for my sins, or if God still had a job for me to do here on Earth. If that was so, what did God want me to do? It took me four years to find out at least some of it.

Chapter Twenty-Two

DREAMS AND PRAYERS

It must have been about two weeks after my hospitalization that I started having recurring dreams. Most of the dreams were about catastrophes and would wake me up in the night, dreams of earthquakes, floods, and fires. They just came, one right after the other. If I dreamed about an earthquake, I would have the same dream two or three times that same week. I couldn't figure out what was going on. I thought maybe it was the medication or that it was just from being weak and tired.

The dreams really bothered me. They kept coming for four weeks. Here's the strange part. If I had a dream about an earthquake, one or two days later I would hear about an earthquake happening somewhere in the world, maybe Turkey or India — somewhere. The same thing happened when I would dream about fires. If I dreamed about a forest fire, I would read about it or hear about it on the news within a day or so. When I had dreams about floods, the dreams were in such detail that I would see people being carried away by the water. I would wake up in a cold sweat wondering where and when these disasters were going to take place. In those dreams, I was always in a safe place during the calamity, like up on a hilltop watching it.

I became very sensitive to these dreams and after I had them, I would become glued to the TV until I saw what I had dreamed about. It was eerie and it was really messing up my mind. I couldn't figure it out. I talked to people that I knew who were experts at analyzing dreams and they couldn't give me an answer, either. This was a terrible thing to have to live with. I thought about Nostradamus and his visions and I actually felt sorry for him and those people that can "see" things. It must make their lives unbearable.

During my recovery I really looked forward to my Reiki family get-togethers. I mentioned before that both Sally and I are first and second degree Reiki therapists. We're part of a wonderful group of Reiki practitioners that get together twice each month and we give each other Reiki treatments. I anticipated those nights because when I was in the hospital, every Reiki therapist in California, possibly the world was sending me energy. It sure felt like it. I think it was partly because of this energy that I healed so rapidly. I'm not taking anything away from modern medicine because I know without it I would be dead today, but I must say that Reiki energy does speed up the healing process. I have talked with many people who had the same problem I had and their recovery time was much longer than mine was. Where it was taking them three months to heal, it took me just five weeks! I have to give credit for my fast recovery to Reiki energy and prayer.

I can't say it too many times — prayer works! You can even feel prayer, especially when you are all alone at night. It's very comforting. All kinds of people were praying for me and sending Reiki healing energy to me as soon as Sally asked them to after my heart attack. I was being bombarded with prayers to save my life and so was Heaven. Thank you to all my family, loved ones and friends. Thank you Leonard and Sylvia Scruggs for notifying all the Reiki family to send me Reiki healing energy. And thank you, my Reiki family for doing so.

I also want to thank all the Earth Angels at Ministry of Prayer in Los Angeles, California, who prayed for me day after day. These are people I have never seen or talked to, and yet they prayed for me. I want to thank all the people who sent Reiki healing energy from around the world, that were asked to do so by my master Teacher, Joyce Morris . . . another group of people that I have never seen nor met.

I also want to thank all the people who helped Sally and me out when we needed it the most and for also giving me encouragement. I'll never forget any of you. You are all very dear to me in my heart and always will be. *And of course the greatest thanks are for You, God, the Father, his Son, Jesus Christ, and the Holy Spirit and all of God's Holy Angels and Saints who made my healing possible. I am grateful beyond words.*

Chapter Twenty-Three

GRUMPY OLD MEN

I have come to the conclusion that there is a different person in my body than the one that lived here before I died and returned. Many changes have taken place in my character. My thoughts have changed. My values have changed. I now realize that life is *the most precious gift from God* there is, and that we should begin each day by saying, "Thank you Father God for this wonderful life and this beautiful place to live it."

After my first flush of renewed awareness of God's green world following my coronary thrombosis and my near-death experience, my days became boring and monotonous. All I had to look forward to was taking my walks and my medication. I felt that if I didn't change my routine, I would go crazy.

One day I got in my car and took a drive. I ended up at a large gambling casino on the other side of town. The games they play are legitimate and legal gambling games in the state of California. They play California low ball and Texas hold 'em.

I walked in and looked around. There were six tables all full of players and many gamblers waiting to get in on the games. But I had seen that one table had one open seat and I told the man running the establishment that I wanted to play at that table. The house man asked me if I was sure if I wanted that particular chair because the players were old timers, having played for years together and the youngest one was in his eighties. These were the grumpiest old men he knew of and he couldn't figure out why I would want to play with them. No one else did!

I told him I didn't know why but I wanted that table. A few minutes went by and my name was called and I was told that my seat was available. I bought some chips and sad down to the game. I kept my mouth shut because I wanted to hear the table talk. The houseman had been right. I never heard these guys say one good thing about anyone or anything during our first hour of play. I sat there quietly and won five good hands in a row. This got their attention. Let me give you a brief description of these guys. Unshaven for maybe a week, they needed haircuts, their clothes were wrinkled, half of them wore no socks and two of them were wearing slippers!

I spent the whole afternoon playing cards with these dudes and listening to their negativity. I stayed very quiet and had little to say, but I kept winning pot after pot. I found out that these old men were widowers and this was the reason why they were so grouchy — their wives had departed this life before them! I also found out that they were all at one time professional people. Two of them had been attorneys, one was a retired judge, another a retired doctor, one a retired dentist and one was a retired college professor. It was very depressing for me to sit there and listen to all their negativity, but I wasn't about to leave, since I was winning all their money. When I decided to cash out, I thanked them and told them that it was a pleasure playing with them. I said, "I'll be here at 9am tomorrow morning if you want to get your money back." I thanked them again, then left, returning the next day as I had promised. We gambled like this for several days, each day just like the other, and I would walk away a winner. I was still very quiet at the table and I just listened to their conversations. On the fifth day of playing there was a different attitude at the table. The judge that always sat directly across from me asked what I was wearing on my collar.

Sally had bought me a gold Angel pin and I always wore it on my shirt collar. Everyday I wore my Angel pin everywhere I went. I replied "It's an Angel pin." He asked if this was why I was so lucky and I said no way. My pin wasn't a good luck piece. I wore it to show my appreciation for everything the Angels did for me. He thought that was funny and wanted to know just what they had done for me lately . . . "Have ya won the lottery yet?" I explained that just a few weeks prior to meeting them that my life was saved but "you guys don't want to hear about that." Silence fell over the table. The doctor was shuffling the cards and he said that *he* wanted to hear about it, and then the rest of them agreed that they also wanted to hear about it. I said I would tell them, but if my story became too boring, to please stop me. That was fine with them.

So I started telling them about my coronary thrombosis and how the Angels helped get me to the hospital. I told them all about my near-death experience and that I was living proof that there really is life after death. I told them of the Kingdom of Heaven and the great unconditional love so great that it just overwhelms you. I told them that death was painless and that you cross over into a different realm and how wonderful it feels to finally return home. I explained that we are just visitors here on Earth and that we all started in Heaven. I kept waiting for them to stop me, but they were hanging on every word. I explained how God or the Angels took over when I was speaking to them and I just kept talking and they continued to listen for about an hour.

The judge just kind of stared at me and said "I'll be damned, I thought when you died that was all there is." I said "Not true. Believe me, there is life after death." Then they started asking me questions. Thank God I was able to answer them. The game broke up and I went home.

The next day was Sunday and I stayed home. On Monday, I got up, affixed my Angel pin to my collar and headed for the card room. When I walked in I got a huge surprise. Looking over at our table I could hardly recognize these guys. They were cleaned up, wearing suits and ties, clean shaven, hair neatly trimmed and every one of them had gone out and gotten an Angel pin and was wearing it on the lapel of his suit.

I guess my lecture on just how precious every day of your life is, really got their attention. In the next few weeks these old guys were flying all over the country visiting their sons and daughters and their grandchildren! These old gentlemen will never be the same as they were when I first met them and neither will I.

As word spreads, one person tells another until everyone gets the word. I guess those old timers told most everyone they knew about my near-death experience and the messages I returned with. The story spread and in a short amount of time, the younger, troubled people were coming to me asking

All sorts of questions and telling me their stories. Most of them were really down on themselves due to drug problems. They were all sick and felt unloved. I told them how much God loved them regardless of how they felt about themselves. I told them how important they were in God's eyes. And I told them about their Angels and how to talk with them.

I guess, in total, I talked to about forty or fifty of these lost youngsters. I've heard good news about a lot of them. Four of them are currently in rehab trying to break their drug problems. About five of them got jobs and went to work. Two young runaway girls went home to their parents. I definitely made a difference out there and I couldn't be happier. I don't want to give you the impression that I hang out at places like this all the time. I know that to the good Christian, gambling is a sin. But the people in church don't need my help. I always try to make a difference *everywhere* I go, regardless of where I am.

Chapter Twenty-Four

VISIONS

On August 18, 1997, I walked out to my front balcony and was pleased to see that the full moon was very bright and the sky was exceptionally clear. Venus was supposed to be very close to the moon that night. There was only one problem. I couldn't see the planet Venus. In it's place I saw a giant hole in the sky that I could see through. Inside the hole it looked like there was an island of different colored lights . . . red, blue, green, white, aqua, orange, and so forth. It was a beautiful vision. In the center of the island were tall green skyscraper-like buildings, except instead of looking exactly like buildings, they looked like crystals, very similar to coming into New York Harbor and seeing the New York skyline, except all these buildings were emerald green and they radiated so much color. I rubbed my eyes, shook my head, opened my eyes and closed them again, but no matter what I did the vision was still there. I was wondering if I was developing an eye problem. No matter what I did, the vision persisted. I was transfixed and just stared up at the vision for about fifteen minutes.

I finally was able to tear myself away and go back into the apartment yelling for Sally to come look at the sky. I asked her what she saw. She looked up and said, "I see stars and the moon, with Venus almost right next to it." I asked her what else she saw. She said, "Nothing." I asked her if she saw anything else at all—any lights, maybe? She said she only saw what she had told me . . . the moon and the planet Venus. I told her what I saw . . . just describing it as "lights." We started checking another part of the sky. I saw stars . . . airplanes . . . the trees on the lawn . . . the street . . . cars going down the road, etc. But when I looked to where Venus was supposed to be, there was the hole and the beautiful island city.

We went back into the apartment and Sally made me look at the television to see if I saw any lights in front of it. I only saw the TV. We went back outside and the vision was still there but I was the only one that could see it. We came back in. As the evening progressed, I kept going out and the vision was still there. Around 10:30, I went outside one more time and I was relieved that the vision was gone. I believe this was a Monday night. I checked on the vision again on Tuesday night and it was not there.

Nothing Wednesday, either. I checked on Thursday night and *oh God — it was back!*

From that point on I have always been able to see it except when it's cloudy or when Venus goes below the horizon. There are certain times of the year when the earth's rotation around the sun keeps it out of sight as well. Sometimes the vision changes. It will be turned a little. There also is a huge red cross in there.

That Thursday when it reappeared I went over to my good neighbor John and he came out and he couldn't see anything other than what Sally saw. Our friend Mark arrived and he couldn't see the vision either. Our friends Heidi Ann and Rob showed up but failed to see it. We went to our Reiki meeting and there are many people who are Reiki that have many spiritual talents and are very knowledgeable. Well, none of them could see my vision. They did give me one good piece of advice, however. They told me to enjoy it and possibly I might start to receive messages.

A week later, Sally was in a bookstore and noticed a book entitled, *The Messengers*. The book was about a man named Nick Bunick. On page 77 of that book he tells about a vision of a band of lights that is going to circle the world. They would be multicolored and would be seen around the time of the millennium by everyone.

Sally was overjoyed to see this and read it to me. That night I went out to look at the vision, but at that point no lights had started to extend outward.

At the end of September and early October we went to visit our son, Dean and his wife Darla, who live in Las Vegas, Nevada. The second night we were there we drove way out in the desert, far away from the lights of Las Vegas. The vision was fantastic that night. Shortly after I read *The Messengers*, I had started to notice the lights starting to extend from the ends of each side of the vision, as the book stated that they would, shortly before I left for Las Vegas. This night I noticed that the lights were really starting to extend, becoming longer and longer on each side of the vision. I still have not found anyone who sees this particular vision, but I'm sure, everyone in the world will see it someday. After a week of enjoying Dean and Darla and also visiting our former daughter-in-law, Linda, and our teenage granddaughter, Cherrié (we didn't get to see our grown grandson, Jackie, as he was working), who also live in Las Vegas—we flew to Ontario, California. From there we drove to visit our son Jeff and his wife Kelly and our teenage daughter, Amber and our grown grandson, Bobby and our last grandchild, Jason. They all live in Temecula, California . . . or did then, as they all live in Missouri now, except Bobby, who married his Maria and lives and works in Riverside, California.

Temecula is between Riverside and San Diego. They lived out in the country away from lights, they didn't even have streetlights and that gave me a pristine view of the heavens. I found myself sitting outside for two and three hours almost every night of our stay, just staring up at my vision. There were times that I could see little white lights flying between the tall green crystal-like buildings. I couldn't see what the lights were or what they were doing, but I could see some type of movement. Sometimes the center of the circle turned lavender blue or the vision would be slightly at a different angle. It was simply spellbinding.

After coming home from our trip, I started to see a second vision in the sky. It was mostly white lights at first, but then the colors started coming. It seemed to be located where the North Star is, but as in the case of Venus, I cannot see the star, just the vision. This one started out just like my original vision, and then after several months I couldn't see it anymore. It was almost like it was a reflection of the first one—*Awesome!*

Through the winter months I couldn't see the first vision as much because of the clouds. We experienced a very rainy year because of El Nino and I could not see the vision for long periods of time. I put it out of my mind as best I could because I couldn't find anyone who could tell me what I was seeing. I found that I really missed seeing it when it was obscured by clouds. I want it to *be* there, it is so very beautiful.

Today, in 1999, the first vision is still very clear when I see it. The second vision returned this spring with stunning clarity and is *huge*! It is just like the first vision but it is so very astounding. The lights now expand from horizon to horizon and there are so many colors! I am told everyone will see these lights someday, as they will extend all around the world. Isn't that fantastic?

What was *not* so beautiful during these winter months, was the return of more terrible dreams and I was afraid to go to sleep because I thought that I might not wake up. These were not normal dreams at all. They had sounds and smells that were absolutely real and the feelings they gave me were too intense. It was just like being there, not dreaming it, but living it. I started writing these dreams in my journal because I was hoping that one day a dream analyst could help me out with them. I haven't found anyone yet, but I haven't given up hope.

One January night I dreamed that it was dusk and Sally and I had just walked out of a large store where we had been shopping. We left through a revolving door and I could not see; my eyes were tearing up and watery from the smoke and fire everywhere around us. I could hear people screaming and crying and I could hear sirens in the distance. I heard broken glass falling everywhere. I was groping in the dark for Sally's hand and I could barely see her. We got out of the building and I tripped over three or four dead bodies in the street. A loud, clear voice came through the smoke and fire. It said, *"Glenn and Sally, do not fear. I am with you. Look to your daily prayers."* I woke up sweating in bed and tried to figure out what this was all about. Then I remembered that everyday, without fail, I pray the 91st Psalm, which is the Psalm for protection. There is a part in the Psalm that says, *"A thousand shall fall at thy side and ten thousand at thy right hand, but it shall not come nigh thee. Only with thine eyes shalt thou behold and see the reward of the wicked."* I thought that this could be a part of this Psalm.

These dreams of destruction and terror went on for a long time. There isn't any point in telling you about each and every one of them, but they all had more catastrophes in them. They were terrible and eventually they slowly stopped coming, to my extreme relief. There have been a few more in a similar vein but nothing anything like I experienced previously.

***

I have one other vision unlike any other, one that left me considerably shaken. It occurred on my daily walk around the golf course. The temperature was cool, but not cold. There were beautiful white, cotton ball clouds in the sky and the wind was diminishing. I had been walking for about thirty minutes when I noticed the sky was getting darker. I thought it might be getting ready to rain so I turned for home. I stopped near a very large oak tree and checked the sky. The clouds had now hidden the sun from my viewpoint and I noticed the clouds starting to swirl around in a strange way, like a whirlwind, moving very fast but the clouds remained very white, which I also thought was strange, as the sky remained quite dark.

Very quickly, the white clouds started to form into a beautiful man. First the face formed. I could see his eyes, nose and mouth. His hair was a little past shoulder length and was parted in the middle. He had a neatly

227

trimmed beard, which came to a point. Then his body started to take shape. He wore a long white robe and his hands were clasped together in front of him. This was happening very quickly, as I said before. Then the sun seemed to radiate behind him and sunbeams were shining from him. I watched, rooted to the spot.

He began to speak and his voice was very deep and the sound it made thundered in my ears. He spoke to me very slowly, deliberately and clearly. I knew the words were directed only to me. The message was astounding! Here is what I heard:

"Stay close to me, but do not rush to join me in my realm, for I will always be in your world with you. Long ago you agreed to be born into your world to complete a task I have asked of you. It was a promise to me and a promise is a contract. You will join me only when this task is completed and not before. This you call your destiny. You are doing well. I love you."

As the words drummed into my ears, my knees literally gave way. I found myself sitting on the grass with my hands covering my ears to try and diminish the volume of this thunderous voice.

I sat there under the oak tree with tears streaming down my face. I was weak and shaking like a leaf. I had to sit right there for quite awhile before I regained strength enough to make it back home. Upon entering my home, I immediately went to bed and slept like the dead.

When I awoke, I realized that it was God's will that I be here to do some kind of work I had agreed to do, knowing that I would be directed as to what I am to do. Even though I still wanted to be "back home," the depression I had been feeling was gone.

I felt that it was God or Jesus speaking to me. I was deeply humbled. Unfortunately, the depression returned for a couple of weeks before it disappeared. Deep in my soul I had a longing to feel the wonderful unconditional love I had felt in my near death experience. I missed the peace and solitude . . . the beauty that was there. I was dismayed at being sent back to the Earth plane, with all its confusion and despair. I just wanted to "go home" and home to me was there, not here.

Chapter Twenty-Five

MEETING ANGEL RUTH

I have some friends who are spiritually gifted and one of the things they are blessed with is the ability to see auras. An aura is the glow of energy that all living things have around them. People's auras can have many colors. Some people's auras are very bright and other people's auras can be dull I am told. People with dull colors are usually very ill people, or people that are not spiritually aware in any way.

On February 25, 1998 I was sitting at a table outside, enjoying a cup of coffee in front of a donut shop. This donut shop is on the corner of a small shopping center. I was facing the sun. I'd been there a few minutes when a lady and two children came around the corner of the building. The sun was behind them. The lady looked like she was maybe 37 years old. She was at least four or five inches over six feet tall, very statuesque and very beautiful. She was slender and quite graceful. She had very soft, brilliant, shining, straight long jet-black hair, which was swept around to one side, hanging down the front of her body. It looked as though she had combed it straight back and just let it fall naturally without any attempt to part it. Her face had regular features, a very slender, straight nose, and a well-formed mouth with beautiful white teeth. She seemed to be smiling even when she wasn't smiling. Her skin was a rich brown and she might have been a native of India. What was really arresting about her was her very high cheek bones and her eyes which were very large and very green — soft and full of love, and kind of slanty like a cat's eyes. She was striking . . . very striking. She was not a person you could easily forget. Very unusual. She was wearing a soft, lime green long dress, with a sash around it. The sleeves were long and loose fitting, very causal. She wore no jewelry of any kind and the green gown complimented her green eyes.

The little boy and little girl were white. Both were blond. The little girl had long, straight hair. The little boy's hair had a standard haircut, very neat and parted on the side. His hair was also straight. They were both wearing identical soft orange plaid tee shirts. The little boy wore blue jeans and tennis shoes. The little girl was wearing pink slacks and pink tennis shoes.

What *really* got my attention was a 3 to 4 foot wide shimmering, pure white light that surrounded this lady and this light extended a little past her knees. It was mind-boggling! I was so excited that I could finally see an aura! She passed me and went into the donut shop. I was so amazed at seeing her incredible aura that I followed into the donut shop. There I was in the shop, literally gaping at her with my mouth open. I finally realized what I was doing and got a hold of myself and went back to my table outside.

Shortly after that she came out of the donut place and it looked as though she was leaving, but instead she turned around and asked me, "May I ask why you were looking at me that way in the shop?" I was very embarrassed, but excitedly said, "I can see your aura . . . I've never seen an aura before and yours is so beautiful. It's white." She said, "I can see yours, too. Yours is gold." (My friends who can see auras have told me this also.) I then asked her about what she did and she answered, "I take care of underdeveloped children." The children that she was accompanying seemed quite normal and were very well behaved. I remember thinking that it was an unusual occupation and I didn't really understand what she did, but I didn't pursue it. Instead I said, "I really would like to talk to you someday." She answered, "Oh, we will talk and I will see you soon." She laughed a little and smiled and then walked away with the children and went around the corner of the building and was gone. I had no idea that this was my dear Angel Ruth. I just thought that she was a beautiful, unusual person.

After she left, I realized that I could smell the fragrance of fresh carnations. It was not an overpowering aroma, yet I was very aware of it and it was refreshingly pleasant. I smelled that fragrance for the rest of that day and clear into the next! I thought that was unusual, but didn't really think about it too much.

I kept going back to the donut shop, waiting for her to come and talk to me, as she said she would. One full week went by and I did not see her. By now, I was starting to miss her.

On the eighth day, I went back to the donut shop and decided to buy a newspaper. It was a beautiful morning for a February day. It was even warm. The time was around a quarter past ten and I didn't see anyone around, which was pretty unusual for that time of day. The shops had all opened at ten and yet, as I said before, the parking lot was completely devoid of people.

I was unconsciously keeping my eye out for the lady who smelled like sweet carnations, but at the same time, I was enjoying my stroll. I noticed that a new gun shop had opened and was advertising their grand opening. I thought, "That's all we need — another gun shop —

when there are so many guns on the street already and gangs don't mind using them and causing such a lot of everyday violence. Why would anyone want to open another gun shop?"

So no one was around me. The parking lot was still completely empty of people and all of a sudden the lady just materialized right next to me. There is no way that she could have walked up to me. BAM! She was *just there*, right by my side. I turned to look at her. I had to look up at her; she was so much taller than I am. I am only five foot ten and as I said before she is well over six feet tall.

I was very startled and I couldn't figure out where she came from. But I had my wish. This was the same lady who's aura I had seen. She said to me in a very cheery, soft voice with a hint of mirth in it, "Good morning, Joshua." I told her that my name was Glenn Maxwell. She looked at me and laughed and said that she knew me as Joshua. My hair on the back of my neck stood up and I thought maybe I was talking to some nut case, but I decided she seemed harmless enough. Then she reached over and put her hand gently on my shoulder and then removed it. When she did this, my knees turned to water. I had to lean up against the building (I was walking on the sidewalk and not in the parking lot) to keep from collapsing.

The energy that came out of her hand was too much for me to handle. When she took back her hand, she looked into my eyes and asked, "Are you ready?" A voice came out of me that wasn't my own and I had no thought as to what I was saying, but I heard this new voice of mine replying, "I've been ready since the beginning of time." (She continued to look into my eyes.) "Is He coming?" and she responded "Yes". I then heard myself ask, "When?" and she replied, "Soon...and be prepared." Then I asked, "What should I do?" She answered that I would be told what to do and that she would be with me.

There is an alley that goes through the shopping center that connected one street to the other. This guy by the name of Frank came around the corner. Frank is a homeless man, but always friendly. He came up to me and asked me for a cigarette. I gave him a cigarette hoping he would leave quickly so I could continue talking to this woman. He took off walking across the street and I remember turning back to the lady and my own voice returned to me and I said to her, "I don't see your aura today." She said, "Oh, I just used that to get your attention last time." Then I happened to glance into a reflection in the window for a split second and when my gaze returned to where she had been, *she was gone!*

Just like that! Gone! I was flabbergasted . . . stunned! What is this woman? I looked up the alley and around the building. She was nowhere to be seen. She had vanished into thin air.

I was kind of feeling sick and my knees were trembling. I felt like as though a bolt of lightning had hit me. I felt a chill go through my body and I thought that just perhaps I was losing my mind.

I walked to a nearby Asian restaurant and asked for a glass of water. I sat down for a minute because I was still feeling queasy. I was trying to get my head back to normal and I was shaking like a leaf. I could hardly move. The restaurant staff became very concerned about me, but I told them I would be all right. They even asked if I needed an ambulance. I finally got myself together enough to leave the restaurant and go on my way, when I spotted Frank, whom I had given the cigarette to.

I managed to walk over to him and I asked him if he knew the lady I was talking to when he came by and bummed a cigarette. He said, "Uh, yeah, Glenn. I remember you giving me the cigarette, but there was no woman with you. There was nobody with you. Believe me, if there had been a woman there I never would have bothered you. I would have remembered that." I just shook my head and got in my car and managed to drive home. On the way home I had time to reflect on what had happened. I recalled that the woman was not as dark-skinned as she had been when I first saw her and this time she had been wearing a long soft white dress, loose this time, with long full sleeves, like a choir robe.

I was lucky not get into an accident, I was so anxious to tell Sally about this encounter. As I rushed home, I recalled that before the lady appeared and for about fifteen minutes afterward I smelled the fresh fragrance of carnations. Then I started thinking about the voice that came out of me when I first started talking with her. It was a deep authoritative voice. It was in a way, earthshaking but definitely not mine. It really scared the hell out of me. Who was this woman? When would I see her again? And I was already longing to see her once more.

Three long weeks went by without a glimpse of her. Every now and then I could smell the fragrance of the carnations, and I would get very excited about this but I saw and heard nothing. But she hadn't deserted me. Our next encounter took place on March 26, 1998 at 8:05 in the morning. I had an appointment on the other side of town and as I left the house I gave Sally a kiss goodbye and after she placed a Reiki shield around me for protection, I got into the car and drove to my appointment.

Every morning that's our routine. Sally and I give each other Reiki protection for the day in order to keep all negativity away from our bodies. As I drove slowly down our residential street, being careful of the school children crossing back and forth, I started smelling carnations again and then heard a very clear, soft feminine voice that asked, "How do you wish to be addressed?" At first I thought it was coming from my radio. I reached down to turn the volume up on the radio and realized the radio was not on. Again, the voice repeated the question, only louder. There was no one in the car except me. So I thought I may as well answer the question and hoped no one noticed me talking to myself. I said, "I am known as Glenn, and my full name is Alfred Glenn Maxwell, but I prefer the name Glenn." The voice answered me "I like Alfred and will address you as Alfred, your true given name." By this time I realized I was swerving all over the road and I needed to pull over to a nice quiet place so I could try and make some sense out of this voice and the fact that I was actually answering its questions!

The disembodied voice was coming through so clearly, as if someone was sitting right next to me in the car. I looked at my watch and it was 8:10am. I pulled over and parked in a quiet place by the river. I asked the voice "Who are you and what do you want?" She said, "First, I want to tell you that I am very proud of you because of your increase in spirituality. You have always been a good man, but never very religious or spiritual. You have always loved God, but very seldom go to church. My name is Ruth and I am your spirit guide. You have other Angels with you at all times, but I am chosen as the speaker." She explained to me that there are no accidents or coincidences. She went on to explain that I had a job to do and that my life was going to change abruptly and very rapidly. She continued, saying that there are people who have been chosen to work with God during the Millennium and that this was a very large network of people. She gave me a figure of 144,000 in the first "wave." I didn't understand what this meant, but she explained that I, along with the others, was to prepare for the Millennium. She said that my Reiki powers would be increased a hundred-fold and that her reason for talking to me on our Earth plane was because I cannot meditate properly. This is certainly true, because I have never been able to quiet my mind long enough to meditate. My circle of life is surrounded by too much confusion and she was unable to break through to me via meditation. She said that I needed to stay on the path I was following and to stay close to the light energies and avoid the dark energies, as they are evil. We talked about other things that I can't remember, but she did say that she would work with me and soon I would be able to hear her messages more clearly. She wanted me to be open to her voice.

I decided that if this entity or light being, or Angel, or whatever, was going to come into my life and practically take over, that I had better find out if she was an Angel of God or possibly an agent of Satan. I did not know and I wanted to find out for sure.

I asked her if I could ask some questions of her. She said I could ask her anything I cared to, but for me to be careful of the question because I may not like the answer. She said that there were some questions that she would not answer at all because the answers were not for me to know at that time. Well, I was prepared, so I asked my questions and here are some of her answers:

Q. Why did you pick me, why was I chosen?
A. I didn't, it was God's choice.

Q. Isn't there someone else that is more qualified to do God's work than I am?

A. You have been chosen. You have the proper spiritual DNA.

Q. I don't understand, what's spiritual DNA?

A. Some people have it. It is an opening in the spirit that allows God's Angels through to your realm, or world, to do our work there.

Q. What will I be expected to do?

A. Whatever God wants you to do. He will tell me, then I will tell you and we will do it together. I will always be here for you.

Q. Can you turn down your energy when we are together? Your energy is making it difficult for me to breathe, move or do anything.

A. Yes, I can do that. We will adjust.

Q. I'm not sure I believe all this. Maybe I'm hallucinating or something.

A. This is real. God has much for us to do. This is the reason you were sent back to Earth. You must finish your job here. You will keep a journal of our meetings. I will be giving you information and you will write it in your journal and at the proper time, release it to the world. You will undergo many tests of your sincerity before we begin our work together. I will show you how to contact me and I will show you how I will get your attention.

Do not worry or be afraid because I love you very much just as God loves you. The work that we will be doing is very important in the scheme of things to come.

Q. What I saw when I died, was it all real or just my imagination?

A. You have only seen a small part of the Kingdom of Heaven. Yes! What you saw was very real. Please tell me what you remember seeing as most people have blockages of their experiences.

So, I told her of the city and all that I had seen of the countryside, the oceans, beaches, animals, and the beings I had seen. Ruth informed me that what I had seen was what we know as Paradise. Paradise is what you believe will happen to you and where you will go after death. Each individual might believe this personal paradise to be different from someone else, so everything must be what he or she believes in.

Whatever you believe your paradise to be, it will be that way. I told her about the vision I saw in the sky and Angel Ruth told me it is always there to remind me of where I once was.

And it *is* always there. Every time I look up, it's there. At first I thought it was just a thing of beauty that I was permitted to see, but as the blockages of my near-death experience started to dissolve, I realized that this vision that I see is a part of what we refer to as the Kingdom of Heaven. The whole structure is the same, the colors are the same, the buildings are the same, but they are just much farther away than they were when I first saw them.

Ruth said if I would have stayed in the Kingdom of Heaven any longer, I would have undergone a life review, but very few return after being in Paradise that long. At a life review, qualified beings sit and review your life from birth to death. They look for events in your life that could have been handled better or to see where you succeeded or failed in certain episodes of your life. This is not designed to degrade you or to reward you. Life here on Earth is a learning event. Life review is designed to find out if you learned anything while living your life and to point out the mistakes you made along the way. After my review I would have discussed these events with the entities in charge. I would have then been taken to a place to rest for as long as I needed. At this juncture, I would have had the opportunity to consider being reincarnated, in hopes of doing better next time.

Ruth said that in the process of being reincarnated we can select our mothers and fathers while still in our spirit form and be born into the family we choose. It's a simple procedure. You make the choice to be reincarnated and after the body of the baby is formed in the mother, at the very moment of birth your spirit enters into the baby's body and at its first breath you will have been reincarnated or reborn to start a new life. It's very similar to the procedure I went through when I was sent back to re-enter my body in the intensive care unit at the hospital.

She then told me that the reason I saw no sun in the Kingdom of Heaven is because Heaven is illuminated by the Light of God! I came to the conclusion that Ruth can only be one of God's Angels because after she left, I felt that my entire being was enveloped with pure, overwhelming love, and anything that is pure love can only come from God the Almighty. I have learned through my near-death experience that the most powerful law on Earth is love, and love is the only law in Heaven.

I sat there for a few minutes trying to gather my thoughts and what this really meant and after awhile the fragrance of the carnations went away. It seemed as if I had been there for about 5 minutes speaking with Angel Ruth. I looked down at my watch and it was ten thirty. I had missed my appointment and I had lost a little over 2 hours of time!

Chapter Twenty-Six

ACTING ON A VISION

On April 15, I awoke abruptly and it seemed like I was right at the end of a dream or was listening to music, and there were words that stuck in my head the way the words in a song will do. I got up and started getting ready for the day. While I was in the shower these words stuck in my mind and kept coming out like a song. The last words of the song were "be one with the flame." This didn't make any sense to me so I kept trying to put it out of my mind and go on about my business.

My back had been bothering me for awhile and when I came home that evening, I told Sally about my back pain and she gave me Reiki and the ache lessened but was not completely gone. Sally told me to take a hot bath because maybe I was having a muscle cramp and the hot water would relax the muscle. This made sense to me. Sally then turned out all the lights, unplugged the telephone and lit a candle. Because I had been under pressure so much recently with the appearance of Angel Ruth and what all this meant, she wanted me to just relax, get some peace and quiet and soak in the tub until my mind was clear.

As I lay in the tub totally relishing every peaceful moment, I noticed the candle flame flicker and suddenly a fragment of the song came back to me, "be one with the flame." I began staring into the burning wick of the candle or rather I was looking slightly above it, when all of a sudden a flash of brilliance like a strobe light hit my face. I saw a vision of myself sitting on a rock, out on a point looking out at a lake. I thought, "So much for clearing my mind," and I continued to sit in the tub, confused by this new occurrence. Suddenly, another flash and a larger scene of me on the rock and a very large lake which contained an island. It still didn't mean anything to me and then the flash fired again and I saw the entrance to the lake. There was a gate and on the gate there was a large clock that had the day of the week and the time of the day. The clock read Wednesday, 3pm. That day and time kept flashing in front of my face. I realized then that I recognized the lake and had been to that same place many times. But I didn't remember any clock. All day long I had the feeling that I should drive to the lake which is about 80 miles from our home. I was simply compelled to go.

And the next morning I went. When I got to the lake, it was cold outside and there was still snow on the ground. It was cloudy and it felt like any minute another storm would start. But I was compelled to be there, at the lake, right at three o'clock. I pulled through the gate at 2:30 and drove down to the boat docks. I drove all around the lake and, as I drove, the water was always in my view with the exception of one area where the road goes up a hill and the pine trees are so tall that the lake is momentarily obscured from view. I still didn't understand why I needed to be there, but I just knew I had to be.

I only saw two people while I was driving. One man was on the boat dock with his fishing line in the water. Another man was walking toward the dock and he was carrying a fishing pole. Snow completely encircled the lake, but it wasn't snowing at the time. Clouds were starting to form for another storm.

I had my heavy winter jacket on and I walked out to a point overlooking the water. I sat there for quite some time and nothing happened. The clouds were getting blacker and ready to let loose and shortly it started to snow. I thought to myself, "Here I am sitting out on some dumb rock by a lake in the middle of a snow storm". I looked at my watch and it was

2:55. I thought for a minute and knew, for whatever reason, I was supposed to be here but if nothing happened by three o'clock, I would leave. I had parked on a hill with a long path and figured that if I didn't take off soon, it would be difficult to get back to my truck in the storm.

By 3pm the snow was falling so heavily that I actually became worried about not making it back to the truck. I started walking up the hill, trying to find the pathway in the snow, and as I was walking I heard a slight rustling sound in the bushes below where I had been sitting. I kept walking up the hill slowly, as the snowy ground was quite slippery, and there was the rustling again. I thought it was probably a dog or a rabbit running around the underbrush, but I decided I'd better take a look. I went back down to where I heard the noise and I pulled back the branches and I looked down to find a little girl there who was about four years old. She had a dress on with long stockings and she was very pretty except for the tears that were streaming down her face. She was all scratched up from the bushes she'd been crawling around in. I couldn't believe that some parent would let a little girl out in weather like this with no coat or supervision. I knelt down so I wouldn't frighten her and I asked if she was lost and she nodded her head that she was. I asked where her mom and dad were and she shrugged her shoulders like she didn't know. I picked her up and told her not to be afraid and that I was her friend and that we would go find her mom and dad.

As we made our way back up the hill to my truck, I looked around and there was no one around except me and this little girl and I remembered that when I entered the area, I only had seen the two fishermen. We left my truck and walked about a quarter of a mile when we heard a lot of voices around the area where the lake wasn't visible from the road. I found a pathway that led back down to the lake and as I walked around a large rock outcropping, I could see a bunch of people forming a search party, probably for this same child.

I placed the little girl down on the ground and gave her my finger to hold onto as we made our way up to the search party. I asked if she saw her mom and dad up there in the search party and she said with a huge smile that she *did*. That little sweetheart was so happy and excited to see her folks. We both made our way up the hill and as I got closer to the group of people I shouted "Anybody missing a beautiful, little girl?" The search party and her parents came running down the hill and her mother swept the little girl up in her arms and hugged her fiercely. Everybody thanked me and wanted to reward me but I told them the best reward was just seeing that the baby was reunited with her parents, (and by the way, folks, how about keeping a closer eye on your daughter.)

In the back of my mind I was aware that these people may be thinking that I was trying to kidnap her or something worse and I wanted to deliver that little girl and get the heck out of there as fast as I could. It's terrible the way we live now in constant fear that someone would do anything bad to a little child, but unfortunately this is the way it is. I had made sure that the little girl was with her mom and dad and we didn't exchange names or anything and although they wanted me to stay and have coffee, I just wanted to go home.

I made my way back to my truck and started driving out of the park. Then I got to thinking that had I not been there, sitting on that rock just at the right time, that the only thing between this little girl and the dense forest was me. I decided that this is why I had to be where I was and I felt very good about the fact that I did listen to this "calling" and I did hang around, even in a snow storm, until 3pm. But the best thing was that when I was staring at the open flame of the candle the day before, something opened up in my head. It was very exciting to me that these visions were coming through and I was able to understand that I was needed and maybe this first vision was a test and I had passed the test!

On my ride home, a voice came to me that I had done well and that this little girl was going to play a great part in the Millennium. She is going to grow up and be something very special.

Chapter Twenty-Seven

EXCEPTIONAL FRIENDS

As I reflect back on my life as it was and as it is now, there have been so many changes made it is almost like living a different life altogether. Whereas I used to love crowds, parties, booze and women, I now find myself not being able to stand crowds, I hate confusion and violence, I don't drink at all, and I found my soul mate and need no other personal fulfillment in my life. My friends and closest associates are also changing. At this point in my life, I find myself drawn toward, and being intimate with artists, writers and advanced spiritual people.

Sally became interested in a man named Andy Lakey who was asked to draw 2,000 angels by the year 2000AD. Angels made this request of him. If you are interested in his story, his book is entitled *Art, Angels and Miracles*. We found out that Andy was coming to a store in our area named Angels and Treasures to exhibit his paintings and artwork. Sally wanted to go see him and she wanted me to discuss the visions I was having with him. We went out to see this artist and I did have the opportunity to meet with him. He was a very nice person and was extremely interesting and he appeared to be genuinely interested in the people who had come to see his work. He is an exceptional artist. Since this initial meeting, Andy and I have become friends.

The story of Andy's spiritual awakening is astounding. His book, relating his story and showing many of his paintings of Angels, is wonderful to own and appreciate, and would be a thoughtful gift as well.

One night I called a beautiful and sensitive lady friend of ours and talked to her about my vision. She is a well-known artist and her name is Allison Miner, Ali for short. She paints beautiful Angels and celestial scenes. Her paintings speak to me on a higher plane and have a profound affect on many other people as well. Sally and I have become very close to her and her husband, Al McDaniels. We love Ali's work and her and Al's love of life. I have given her all the information and all the colors (impossible, of course) of my vision that I could lay out on paper and someday she is going to attempt to paint what I see. How I wish I had the talent to do it myself. It will be serious fun to show everyone or attempt to show everyone what I am seeing. No artist in the world could capture the grandeur or the majesty of what I see, but if anyone can even get close, it's Ali. I sure appreciate her attempt and I know when she has the time she will give it her very best shot.

Ali has put out a wonderful book that contains many pictures of her paintings and Angel messages for each picture. It, too, is a beautiful book and the title is *A Time to Awaken.* This book makes a wonderful gift, too.

Another person who had a great impact in my life is a man named Nick Bunick. I have already mentioned him. I've already mentioned the book about him, *The Messengers,* written by Julia Ingram and Gary Hardin. It is all about his spiritual awakening in his middle age, which led him to go into hypnotherapy, which is past life regression. In a past life he was Paul of Tarsus. This is a wonderful book and relates to his time he spent with Jesus. He called him Jeshua. He calls him Jeshua to this day. Nick is a deeply committed man and he is teaching now how Jesus' messages have somehow during the centuries been changed from messages of love to messages of fear and messages of compassion have become messages of guilt. Nick now has written his own book and it is called *In God's Truth.* This is fascinating book also, and I highly recommend it. I feel very connected to Nick and have shared my vision with him and he has also become my good friend.

How fortunate a man can I be to have three such spiritual friends as these? There are many others as well who are special to me and all of us share a close spiritual bond. We share our visions and what is going on with our spirituality. Our conversations are so very, very private that I don't even share them with Sally. These conversations are sacred to me. As I said, I have formed a close spiritual bond with all three, and Andy Lakey and a friend of mine, Richard Welles and I have formed a group that we call The Lakewell Group. We are in the process of preparing a movie of the week of Andy's life story. When this project gets off the ground, it's going to be a lot of work but fun and best of all we'll get to share our friend, Andy with a wider following. The movie is titled, *The Andy Lakey Story.*

The Angel store that Sally and I frequent the most is called Angels and Treasures in the city of Sacramento, California. Diane and Michael Shubin own it. One of the books they sell is entitled, *Andy Lakey's Psychomanteum,* by Keith Richardson. This book is about how Keith and his wonderful wife, Francesca, opened their own Angel store named Things from Heaven and eventually "knew" that they had to sell

Andy Lakey's work. The book tells how the store evolved and then goes into how they made what they call a psychomanteum room in their store. This room contains Andy Lakey paintings.

Andy's paintings are not ordinary by any means. They have healing energy in them and the rest of Richardson's book is about all the miracles that have happened to people who have touched Andy's paintings in their store. It's a wonderful little book and I suggest you buy and read it. The Richardsons are such a nice couple. Their store is in Ventura, California, just below Santa Barbara. The first time I looked at one particular painting of Andy's in the psychomanteum, I immediately started to relive my near-death experience and was reduced to sobbing. Francesca was able to bring me out of it. I went back for another visit and looked at the same painting and it happened exactly the same way as the first time. *Powerful!* (I'm not a man that cries easily, but when it comes to anything connected with God like that, with all that love, well I just go to pieces. It is that wonderful.)

Before we knew it, we created a network of people all interested in the same things, all of us from different walks of life, and this network is a support mechanism for us all. If Andy is having a show in Carmel, as many of us as possible will be there. If I need to discuss what's happening on the screenplay or what's going on in my life spiritually, I know I can count on my network to be there for me. This is a wonderful part of my life, a place where I never thought I would be. I'd never even know that these sorts of people existed. We welcome new folks almost every day into this "network." They are wonderful souls, fully committed, very accomplished in their fields and some are marvelously multi-talented! They make me feel humble, and at the same time, they fill Sally and me with joy. They are all Givers. It looks as though many, many people will be in our "network."

Chapter Twenty-Eight

ANGEL RUTH

Sally received a message just as she was starting to take a nap one day and she knew it was meant for *all* the people in our network, whether they were part of it now or will be at some later time. The message was:

"You are all my beloved children. You have done well. There is much work to be done. It will be made easy for you . . . have fun!"

What a message! It is so hard at times, like getting this book finished, but the helping hands have been unbelievable . . . and I'll admit that most difficulties are being made easy for us. Besides, you can't beat the fun and joy we're getting.

Having this close network has allowed me time to open up to my Angel Ruth. She and I have become so close that she is like a little voice that is sitting on my right shoulder. I hear her so clearly. At first I had to tell her to turn her energy down because it was so intense that it made weakened me to the point that I could hardly stand or talk. Angels carry so much energy with them! I can't explain it, but it can be overwhelming. Angel Ruth talks to me and brings me messages. I can say emphatically that in the last year that we have been together, she has never said anything to me that is wrong. I take my problems to her and she comes up with solutions. She warns me of events that are going to happen. I can always tell when Angel Ruth is near me because the humidity changes. For example, if I'm driving in my car and she needs to speak with me, I can feel the humidity inside the car rise and so I pull over to speak with her safely.

We also have our own little routine. Everyday at sunset during spring, summer and fall, I go for a walk. I live right by a golf course and there is this one place that is absolutely delightful. At sunset, the front nine of the golf course is empty, as all the golfers have finished that section so there is no one there except for my Angel Ruth and me. I sit on the bench and she and I watch the sunset together. She lets me know that this is the time of the day that Angels get their orders from above, meaning she gets her orders from God. She won't tell me anything else except that. We will sit there and have the most wonderful discussions.

Once I asked Angel Ruth if she could tell me more about herself. She replied, "I will tell you all you need to know. I have two responsibilities. One is your well being and the other is the Hierarchy of Adonai Malektt. I will tell you but you will not understand what I am telling you." So she told me and she was right. I didn't understand a word of it.

I researched all I could find on the subject of Adonai Malektt. I found a book written by David Goddard called *The Hierarchy of Adonai Malektt*. The book was about the evolving hierarchy of humanity. The tenth hierarchy is destined to be humanity. At the moment a small percentage of men and women comprise a group that bear various names in different spiritual traditions. The Spiritual Israel, The Great White Lodge, the Company of Just Ones Made Perfect, the College of the Holy Spirit and the Withdrawn Order are some of these groups.

The number of the august body grows from generation to generation and from age to age. They serve as mediators between corporal humanity and the other nine hierarchies of light. It is from these men and women, those who have attained that all true mystery schools receive both their teachings and the vitality for their work. When humanity as a whole has achieved its God-given destiny, it will comprise that which is symbolized by the winged human, the fourth Archon of the Crown, and the whole human life wave will become the tenth hierarchy, the hierarchy of Adonai Malektt.

Because of the faculty of free will, only humanity can choose to love, serve and unite with the One. When this happens, the Creator, as the Quabalah says, will be restored to his throne, which is the human heart. And God shall be all in all.

Angel Ruth informed me that she can only speak or act through me and that I should share her words with everyone I can.

Q. How exactly does one go about walking in God's light? What does it mean?

A. This is not a hard task, just resist evil acts. Stay close to God, not only in your beliefs, but also in your actions. Pray constantly. Help others to get to know God and to love him and to praise him Love one another, as we are all sons and daughters of God. Stay away from the dark energies. Do not be tempted to do things that you know are wrong. Start every day by giving thanks to God for your life, your good health, and your home and for everything you have. Thank him over and over. He likes your praise.

If you are parents, find time to spend with your children. Get to know them and find out what their dreams are. Even if you are not religious, teach your children about God and His constant, everlasting love for them. Teach them that there is a God, teach them to pray and listen to their prayers. Take time for your children regardless of the inconveniences. And remember that babies are God's own Angels and that God has entrusted their care to you, to love and nourish and teach them.

Those who walk in the light of God will survive and live to see the New World in all its splendor. Do not turn your back on the needy and helpless. If you cannot help them financially, at least give them a smile and a word of encouragement. Remember, in God's eyes, they are still his sons and daughters and he loves them as much as he loves you. Even if they have given up on life, remind them that God will never give up on them. Sometimes a word of encouragement means an awful lot to the down and out.

Try to remember this: Live your life by these three simple words:

1. Love
2. Truth
3. Compassion.

Make these words your guide to life and you will be walking in God's light. In the near future, there will be many changes on the Earth, many souls will depart from here and only those that walk in God's light will remain on this Earth to enjoy the new world.

There was a time when I was running into some obstacles putting Andy's movie together and I was sitting on a little bench which overlooks a water hazard that is really a beautiful lake (except for bad golfers) and the sun sets right over the top of it. I was praying to God, thanking Him for my life and everything wonderful around me and I thanked Him for the love of my Sally, family and friends. I asked Angel Ruth if the projects I was working on were worthwhile, or if was I was just spinning my wheels. I wanted to know that if it the movie was going to materialize and work the way I had planned and I asked for some sort of a sign. There was no movement, no voice and no sign. I always know when Angel Ruth leaves because the air humidity returns to normal and this little buzzing in my ear will stop. I could tell she wasn't there, so I just decided to relax and enjoy the beautiful surroundings of this wondrous day.

Shortly, I felt her re-enter my presence and she told me to raise my head and look. I raised my head up and looked into the sun and couldn't see anything, then I looked to both sides and still saw nothing. Angel Ruth said for me to turn around. So I did. What I saw just couldn't be! It had not been raining, yet there was the most beautiful rainbow. It certainly wasn't a typical rainbow! The rainbow had the most vivid colors but instead of being curved and going across the sky it was shaped like a spear and was coming right out of the earth and shooting straight up into the air for thousands of miles. I was so excited, I ran home to get Sally so she could see this "rainbow" and it was still there when we got out back and she was amazed at its shape and how it came from the earth, not the sky. This was my sign.

Thank You, God.

Angel Ruth tells me that she is staying close to me and she is going to help me through the

Millennium because I have a lot of work that needs to be done. She tells me that there will be other people, I won't be working alone, that there are even more wonderful people coming into my life with the same instructions that I will have when the time comes. Regardless of all of the chaos and catastrophes that are going to take place, we will be safe and that I shouldn't worry about it.

My beloved brother, Dutch was like a twin to me. For the first 20 years of my life, I couldn't imagine turning around without seeing him in a room. He'd been very ill for some time and he had a bad heart. He was living with his daughter in a town called Placerville located in Northern California. I tried to see him as much as possible and tried to keep his spirits up. On July 25 at 4:32am I got a buzzing sound in my ear and I awoke to the smell of carnations. By now you know who was with me. Angel Ruth had come with a message for me. She said that my beloved brother Dutch's spirit had just left his body and that he was still on the earth plane and I should know this.

I thought about that for awhile, went back to bed, and a short time after, the telephone rang and it was my sister calling to tell me that our brother had died sometime during the night but they didn't know what time he passed on. I knew. Angel Ruth had been there and she told me when he left. This is how my Angel works with me. The minute the telephone rang, I knew it would be somebody notifying me of Dutch's passing. It is very difficult to let him go; however, I am very happy for him because I know what lies ahead for him, I have been there and I'm absolutely sure that he will be met by all of our loved ones that have died before us. He will not be alone.

Angel Ruth tells me that on the other side they are very disturbed with the quality and type of entertainment that they are showing on television now. The violence, terrorism, and the amount of hours our children are allowed to watch television is appalling. The only thing children see on the tube is violence; it is destroying their young minds. She tells me that this must be changed. She tells me that never before in the history of the world, has there been so much senseless violence: children killing children, mothers killing their children, children killing their parents. Where do you think they get these ideas? They get the ideas not from the books they read at school but from the endless hours that parents allow them to watch television! These horror shows don't show the *consequences* of all that graphic violence. They don't show the mothers, fathers, sisters, brothers, other members of the family and friends . . . how they feel . . . the pain it causes. This can't continue. This is the reason that she is helping me to produce more quality, spiritual television programming. This is why I am working so hard to try and develop a television series with a spiritual nature, to help change the consciousness of the world.

I am writing this in the simplest form that I know. No one should misunderstand its message. For those that do not believe in the power of God, read this twice!

Chapter Twenty-Nine

SURVIVING THE APPROACHING MILLENNIUM

In the beginning, our beloved Father God created the world. He sent His favorite spirits from heaven to co-create this paradise He made for us. He was very proud and loved His creation. It was His favorite work. He then created the human race. We kept multiplying until we overpopulated the world. We have driven some of God's animals to extinction or near extinction. We have covered His paradise with huge splotches of asphalt and concrete. We are smothering Mother Earth.

Man-made chemicals and gases have almost destroyed the ozone belt around Mother Earth. Our industrial plants pollute our rivers and streams and kill our fish. Few seem to care, and it still continues after all these years. I could go on and on about this, but it's so obvious.

Approximately 55 years ago, God gave our scientists a wonderful gift of knowledge. He gave them the ability to harness the atom, a huge source of energy. This energy could have been used for so many wonderful things. But what did we do with it? What did we *do* with this knowledge that He gave us? We used it to build a bomb! Not just any bomb, but a bomb so powerful that it disintegrated two large cities and killed hundreds of thousands of people. Then we went on to build more bombs and weapons with incredible power to destroy. Now there are so many bombs of mass destruction, that they can't keep track of them. Our own government actually doesn't know where some of them are! What if they fall into the wrong hands? There are enough thermal nuclear bombs to destroy the entire human race and possibly the Earth itself in a matter of hours.

We have presented Father God with a problem. He has given us free will and we have abused His gift. Do you think He's going to stand by and watch us destroy his favorite creation? He loves his Earth. He loves the people He put on this Earth. No! He's certainly not going to just watch us destroy the Earth and ourselves. He has just begun His project. He's coming down to do a little remodeling on His Earth and a lot of pruning out of His people. Just like a pruned tree, if you don't belong here and you are subtracting from the power and beauty of the Earth, you will go; it's just that simple.

Major rivers will change their directions. The dry areas of the Earth will become fertile and the deserts will bloom. The frigid zones will become warm. This will be caused by a shift of the Earth's axis. A complete change in the Earth as we now know it will take place. So when you feel the ground shake beneath your feet, and you see the waters run through your office and your homes, or maybe watch your city wash away and crumble don't get too excited, it's just God doing a little remodeling project.

I've been told that in the years between 2000 and 2010 there will be a bad time for Mother Earth and for us that live on her. The rains and snows will fall longer than usual. The major rivers of the world will leave their boundaries, which will cause them to flood heavily populated areas. At one point in the middle of all this flooding there will be a major earthquake. This earthquake will open up the arterial wells below the earth and cause devastation to everything that is in their paths. This is all going to happen in very large areas of the central United States. Similar catastrophes will take place in China, India, Russia and Africa. Europe will be devastated and so will most of the rest of the globe. There will be more than the usual volcanic activity causing earthquakes, floods and fires. There will be a great shortage of food and water and many souls will be making an early departure from our

Earth. There will be great epidemics in places caused by bad food and bad water. In short, there will be total catastrophe.

Angel Ruth tells me that she is staying close to me and that she is going to help me through the Millennium because I have a lot of work to do. She tells me that there will be other people and I won't be working alone. Regardless of all the chaos and disasters that are going to take place, we will all be safe and not to worry.

Once you have become aware of your Angels, you can use them in all aspects of life. All you have to do is to ask them to join you. They are always there with you. They are a part of you and never leave you.

I have told you the worst things that can happen without massive, worldwide prayer. However, I would like to share one of the most wonderful things that will happen to those participating in this heartfelt prayer.

Those who walk among us in "God's Light" will be saved and my visions outline the wonderful life that awaits us. For those without God, there will be only death, pain, suffering and destruction,

I have no way of knowing if we have run out of time or not, but I strongly suggest that everyone who reads this book start their daily prayers with a special prayer for the good of

Mother Earth. Include in that prayer that all of the wrongs that we have done to her be forgiven. Pray for us to be shown the way to get back on the right track.

Now all of these things I'm warning of can possibly be changed, but the only instrument that we have to change these things is prayer! Massive prayer to God for the protection of Mother Earth and massive prayer to change the consciousness of the world!

I know that there is large, even huge prayer groups operating all over the map for world peace and this is wonderful! Nick Bunick started a massive prayer movement, April 4, 1999 at 4:44pm to be followed by prayer on the last Sunday of every month thereafter at 4:44pm. Nick says that the numbers 444 are the symbols of God's love and the beginning of the age of miracles! Please don't wait. *Start praying now!* Remember, *"Let There Be Peace on Earth, Let It Begin With Me."* Pray on your way to work, pray in the bathtub, pray when you do chores. Pray when and wherever you can. These prayers do not have to be long. Just tell God, thank you, often. Believe me, life will get better for every human being on this planet if we all start having talks with our precious Lord. *He loves you to talk to Him . . . any time . . . about anything! It's simply impossible to be a bother to God with even the most trivial prayer. What is important to you is important to*

Him. And what is important to Him is you! Remember that He even cares for the little sparrow and aren't you more important than a sparrow? Know in your heart that God cares more for all of us than our pitiful comprehension of him can ever imagine.

Chapter Thirty

LUCKY FOR A REASON

These are some of the miracles with which Angel Ruth reminds me to show just how loved and protected I am.

When I was in high school, I was attending the Junior/Senior Prom with my girlfriend. There was one senior, a young man who had received a brand new truck for his graduation present. It was a beauty. He invited quite a few of us to go for a ride in it that night. My girlfriend and I went out to where the truck was and I got in the back of it and reached down to help my girlfriend get in, but she refused to get on board. In the meantime, other students were piling in. I reluctantly got out of the truck because it certainly would have been wrong to leave my girlfriend, no matter how badly I wanted the ride. She and I went back to the dance. It was a great party and we were having a whole lot of fun until we heard the news. About an hour after our friends had taken off in the truck, the Highway Patrol came in and announced that our schoolmates had gone over a cliff and every kid who was in that pickup truck was killed. Had I gone for the ride, it would have been my last ride anywhere. I don't remember how many of my schoolmates were in that truck, but there were quite a few. It was a genuine tragedy.

Then there was the night Sally and I were driving on Pacific Coast Highway along the beach at 90 miles per hour and we both saw the same thing, the sedan broadside on the highway, and nothing happened and we are both alive.

How about the *many times* in Korea when I should have been killed, but wasn't?

There was one occasion when I was flying in from New York back to LA. My connection in LA International Airport was a helicopter that flew to Anaheim and then down to Newport

Beach. This was in the early sixties and I was tired. I hadn't really had much sleep for about three days. It was about ten at night. I was standing in line at the airport waiting to get on the helicopter. I left the line to go to the restroom and when I came back the line had grown. I hadn't yet purchased my ticket to get on the helicopter, and I remember that when I came out of the restroom and walked over to the line, I looked at the people in line and all of their faces looked like negatives in a photograph. I rubbed my eyes but that didn't help, they all still looked like negatives. I saw one man who looked normal get in the line and *he* turned into a negative. That did it! I decided that something was wrong. I didn't know what it was, but I didn't want to be on that 'copter. I went to the telephone and called home and I asked my wife, Eve if she would please send the butler to the airport to pick me up, which she did. Well, the people boarded the helicopter and it took off and I went into the bar and had a drink. While I sat waiting for our butler, a special news bulletin came flashing on the TV screen in the bar. The helicopter I had decided not to board had crashed in Anaheim; everyone was killed. I was alive.

One time I was supposed to meet this guy at a bowling alley. At the time I went there, he was playing cards in the bowling alley's card room. I had never been in that bowling alley before. Right after I walked in, looking around for the card room, I heard my name being paged over their loudspeaker. I was wanted for a phone call. Three times the page was repeated. I went to the desk and asked where the phone was and was pointed towards a pay phone on the wall. I walked over to the telephone and was about to pick up the receiver, when all of a sudden gunshots rang out. I picked up the phone and there was nobody on the other end. If I had not stopped to get the phone call, I would have been in the card room when some berserk person came in and shot the place up, nearly killing one card player.

I was playing cards one night; I always stayed late, especially Saturday night, because that's when all the action took place. For some reason that particular Saturday, I decided I didn't want to stay late and something just told me to go home. I got up and left the boys to their game, got in my car, and drove off. The next morning I found out that right after I left, four people came in with shotguns and made everybody lie down on the floor. Then they robbed every one of their money and personal belongings.

Late one stormy night, Sally and I were coming home from our Reiki meeting and our car broke down on the freeway. Both Sally and I asked our Angels for help, as we knew we were in a dangerous situation, helpless on the side of the freeway late at night. One car went past and the very next car pulled over. It turned out to be my Spanish Earth Angels. They were two beautiful Hispanic ladies and not only did they pick us up, they drove us directly to our home. If they had not stopped and picked us up, I would have had to either take Sally with me in the rainstorm and we would have had to walk about two miles to the nearest gas station, or I would have had to leave Sally in the car where she could possibly have been hurt, robbed or killed, while I went for help. We left our car pulled over on the freeway and when we went back the next day it was still there, untouched. A mechanic who is a friend of mine was able to fix it on the spot.

Angel Ruth knows that these incidences are not coincidental and I now know that I am being kept safe for many reasons. I still do not know all that I have to do as the Millennium draws closer as it has not been revealed to me completely yet, but I will be shown in good time. I am sure of it. What is quite plain is that the Millennium will be upon us very, very soon.

After Angel Ruth reminds me of my many narrow escapes, I feel much better about things. Something has always intervened when I have been in danger. Rather than pushing to make things happen, I just try to live one day at a time and things are starting to move much faster now than ever before.

Living in the present moment and staying focused on what needs to be done right now keeps my frustration level at bay. Angel Ruth says that everyone is being put into their places and when they are all lined up then everything will be ready. I'm looking forward to the day when everything I'm working for comes together, but in the meantime, I'm also enjoying being alive!

Chapter Thirty-One

KNOW YOUR ANGELS

All in all, my life after my near-death experience has been great. I have time to work on my journal. I'm meeting the most wonderful people. I've done a little traveling. I get to sleep in when I want to. Our movie project is moving slowly, but we're getting there. Sally's health is good and mine is good, so I guess everything is fine.

I do feel as if the day I returned to my body in the intensive care room in the hospital was the first day of my life. I am determined to do it right this time. I'm sure I have missed the mark many times in the first part of this life. My "new" life, however long as it should last, will be lived under the three basic laws: Love, Truth and Compassion.

Angel Ruth informed me that I should encourage everyone to try to contact his or her Angels. She also said that at this very moment, there are more Angels in the Earth's environs than ever before in its history. They are here for the Millennium. Something wonderful is going to happen, something absolutely wonderful!

For each soul here on Earth, God has assigned from three to five Angels to watch over them and help them through life. They all have different responsibilities guiding us through our life cycles. We have our Spirit Guides, Guardian Angels, and Healing and Teaching Angels. They are with us from birth to death.

By reading this book, you have read how Angel Ruth made contact with me. I can now summon Ruth when I need her and she can contact me in many ways now that I am aware of her presence and am more open to her. She is such a vital part of my entire being now and I love having her with me twenty-four hours a day.

It is important to love your Angels, but do not pray to them. That is wrong. The act of prayer is reserved for God and God alone. Angels are messengers; they work for God. He tells them what to do and they do it. They get their orders every day and they follow those orders to a "T". By understanding Angels and the tasks they need to perform, perhaps we can make their jobs easier.

Angel Ruth has informed me that after man was created, man and Angels worked hand-in-hand to survive on this Earth. God wanted the human race to survive and advance in their evolution. The odds had to be against them. They were not very big. They were not all that strong or fast. They had to compete for their survival like all the rest of the animals on the planet. The only physical thing they had going for them was a larger brain, and God, with the help of his Angels gave them knowledge and the wisdom to know how to use it for their survival.

As the human race grew up to the point where it could take care of itself, the Angels pulled back to let mankind advance their knowledge and to practice the free will that God had promised them. It has been this way for a long time.

Would you like to make contact with your Angels? Let me try and help you through what I have learned from my relationship with Angel Ruth.

Meditation is very important. You must learn to empty your mind of all worries, problems and negative thoughts. This can be difficult, but keep trying until your mind is a blank. Find a quiet place, a place very private so you will not be interrupted. Sit very still and in a soft voice say "Angels, I don't know if you are here with me or not but if you are, you have my permission to enter into my world and make yourself known to me." They will not come into this realm if they are not asked to. Then sit very still and listen. When they come to you, don't expect them to materialize. It takes a great deal of energy for Angels to appear before you and that most of the time the angels don't think that it is necessary to do so. Be aware of something, possibly brushing your cheek, or your hair. You may feel your hair tingle or your scalp begin to itch. You may feel the humidity in the room change abruptly. You may smell the fragrance of something sweet or the smell of roses or some other type of flower. If any of these things happen, you have probably made contact.

If this doesn't work, try what I do that is always successful for me. Fill your bathtub with water, at the same temperature you use when you take a bath. Do not put anything in the tub that has a fragrance because your Angel may make contact with you through the smell of flowers. As you know, my Angel Ruth smells like carnations. At the end of the tub, near where you place your feet, place one candle in a candleholder and light it. Turn the light off in the bathroom and get into the tub. Once in the tub, get comfortable and totally relax. Let your cares and worries slip away. Clear your mind and stare at the flame of the candle. Ask your Angels to join you, as

I've instructed you to do. If the flame of the candle starts fluttering and there is no breeze in your bathroom, you may have made contact.

Invite your Angels to introduce themselves to you. Ask your Angels their names. When the answer comes, be aware that the Angel's voice may come to you and be very loud, but only you can hear it. Ask your Angel to lower its voice. Also be aware that when the Angels come from their realm into yours, they carry so much energy with them that it may have a bad affect on you. It can make you feel weak or nauseous. If you ask them to lower their energy they will.

You may ask your Angels questions, but they may choose not to answer. If you ask them to help you with a problem you may be having and they tell you what to do about your problem, do not delay, but do as they have instructed immediately. They will accept no excuse for your not taking action on their advice. I first met my Angel Ruth on February 25, 1998. It was shortly after that when she advised me about keeping a journal on the things that had happened to me after my near-death experience. I did as I was told, and so many things began to happen that my journal grew quite fat.

Angel Ruth told me that she would give me information to put in my journal and at a given point of time I should put it into a book for publication. She said that she would have the perfect publisher in the perfect place and the book would be published at a perfect time and until that time to keep writing. I did exactly as I was instructed. But then, as the year was growing to an end, I became lax in my promise to keep my journal up to date.

Angel Ruth became very annoyed with me. In the middle of the night I would get that buzzing sound in my ear and I'd know she was near with a message for me. I would wake up and she would appear to be angry because the book wasn't being written fast enough for her. I promised her I would work harder and tried to keep my promise.

Then my editor's ex-husband passed away and she had to be out of town for awhile. I continued to write page after page with pen in hand. I was still taking down the messages I was receiving from Ruth.

The next interruption was the Christmas holidays and that delayed my writing even more. I could tell that Ruth was getting very upset by the delay. Then, when the Christmas holiday passed, I tried to contact Ruth but I could not reach her. The New Year was upon us and I decided there was no reason to send anything out to the publisher because nothing gets done on the first of the year anyway for almost everything closes down for the holidays. I tried and tried to contact Ruth, but she just wouldn't respond. I felt terrible that I had let her down and I knew she was angry with me for the delay in getting the book out. I knew this was why I wasn't hearing from her.

Finally, on the evening of January 3, 1999, I finally made contact with my dear Angel Ruth. She seemed cold and totally disgusted with me over the delay in getting the finished manuscript off in the mail to the publishers. I tried to explain about my editor, Diane and her situation with her ex-husband's death and that nothing happens over the holidays, but Angel Ruth didn't care to hear any excuses. The last thing she said to me was that she had a job to do and she was doing it. I had a job to do and I *wasn't* doing it. Then there was nothing but silence. She was gone.

I felt sick to my stomach. I couldn't sleep so I stayed up all night preparing the manuscript for Diane so it could be typed and sent off to the publishers. The following morning I got up extra early. I showered and shaved and took the typed manuscript and more than fifty handwritten pages and put them neatly into a shopping bag, ran to my truck, put the bag in the passenger seat and drove off. I was going to be early for my appointment the morning of January 4, but I didn't care because I was so excited about finishing the book.

On the freeway, driving to Diane's office, I started getting very hungry. I hadn't had my morning coffee or anything because I wanted to get my manuscript to her. A friend of mine owns a restaurant about ten minutes from where I was going and I decided to stop in and have a bite. I parked the truck in front of the restaurant, put the bag containing the manuscript beneath the dashboard on the passenger side, checked to make sure all my doors were locked, and went in to eat.

I sat down and ordered my breakfast and coffee. After I ate and paid the cashier, I walked out to the parking lot. This entire breakfast took all of twenty minutes or so. When I got out to the parking lot, I saw an empty place where I had parked. The truck was gone. Angel Ruth couldn't have done a better disappearing act. It was nowhere in the parking lot. The truck along with my manuscript, recorded music on tape of an unproduced musical written for Broadway that Sally's father wrote before his death, the latest script of the Andy Lakey story and the music written by Peter Henderson (Sally's brother) for the Lakey project, had vanished! I was completely nonplussed.

After I accepted the fact that my wheels had been stolen, I realized that all my dreams for the future were in that car and the car was gone. Stolen? Vanished? Disintegrated? I didn't know. I went back into the restaurant and called the police to report the truck being heisted. I felt like I wanted to die.

So, let this be a warning for you, an example. Angels couldn't care less about our little problems we have down here and they sure don't care about our holidays. If you make a deal with an Angel, you better stick to it because they have ways of getting your attention.

I was lost, I was sick, I felt I'd let God down, let Ruth down. I'd let myself down because I procrastinated and didn't follow our agreed upon time schedule. I thought of the notes I had put in my notebook and knew that I couldn't possibly continue my writing without them. But I tried. I worked and worked, but still no word from Ruth. On the fifth day of silence, Ruth woke me in the middle of the night and told me she was proud of me for not giving up on the journal. She said, "Remember, I told you that you would be tested". I asked if I would get my truck back and there was no answer, and I felt her energy leave the room.

I am so happy to have Ruth back in my life that that I've stopped worrying about the truck or anything that was in it. Just knowing that Angel Ruth is still here with me and that God loves me is more than enough for me.

One evening I was preparing my bath and looking forward to my hour of meditation and hoping I would make contact with Ruth to gain more information for my journal. I filled the tub with nice, warm water, lit my candle, turned off the lights, and stepped into the water. I submerged myself, closed my eyes, and just relaxed. After a short while I opened my eyes and as I was staring at the flame of the candle, I saw the flame begin to flicker. There was no breeze blowing so I knew Angel Ruth was here with me. I then began to smell the sweet fragrance of carnations and I knew she was there.

I continued staring at the candle and one of those flashes startled me (the same way the incident of the lake with the lost child, only this time the picture she flashed to me was different). It was a huge, barren wasteland with sand dunes and almost totally devoid of life.

The next flash was that same desert only with a rainstorm; clouds, lightning and driving rain. Then she showed me scene after scene of the rains falling so hard on the desert that a great cloud of dust came up caused by so much rain hitting the dry sand. Another flash and the sun was shining through the clouds and beaming down on the rain-soaked sands.

Then the scenes came fast, one right after another. I was shown sprouts of grass beginning to come up out of the sand and wildflowers blooming. Then large irrigation ditches, miles and miles of ditches crossing the former wasteland. Crops were growing all kinds of vegetables, wheat, corn and alfalfa, everything coming up tall and healthy. Large cities and towns with schools and churches were growing by highways that reached as far as the eye could see, and then the images stopped. Nothing.

The fragrance of carnations left the room and I thought "Please Ruth, I don't understand. What does this mean." I poured more hot water in the tub and waited for her return and was rewarded. Soon Angel Ruth's clean sweet fragrance filled the room again and I knew she had returned. I asked her if one day the deserts of the world would become fertile enough to grow food and to sustain human life. Her answer was simply, "Yes". I asked her when this would happen and she replied, "Soon".

I hadn't forgotten that there are no clocks in Heaven and Angel Ruth's answer to any "when" question is always, "Soon". But can you imagine seeing large cities and towns springing up where practically nothing can survive today? If this happened, two huge problems for the human race would be eliminated. There would never be hunger in the world and no more overpopulation. *"There will be many changes in our world but do not fear. Rejoice and look forward to a shiny new tomorrow."* (Angel Ruth)

As I told you before, on the fourth of January my car was stolen. On the night of January 22, Angel Ruth came into my sleep like a dream sequence in a movie. I saw two young men drive away in my truck. They were real professional car thieves. After they were about three miles from where the truck had been stolen, I saw the truck stopped in the back of a building where there was a large Dumpster. I saw one of the young men, the one on the passenger side, open the door and take out the bag with the tapes and the handwritten manuscripts in it. He lifted the top of the Dumpster and threw away the bag. But the driver had the typed part of my manuscript stuck into his jacket.

I then saw them drive to a large apartment complex where the passenger got out of the truck and the driver sped off. I saw my truck being pulled into an alley behind a large building and parked. It was raining hard and the driver turned on the dome light and began reading my manuscript. When he finished reading it, he thumbed back to one section and re-read it. It was the part that said God never gives up on you even if you give up on yourself. I could see him sitting there for a long time, just thinking about what he had read. While he was pondering my written words, he was also staring at a plaque that was on the dashboard of my truck. The plaque had a picture of Jesus and written below it was, "God protect us in our hour of travel." He then started the truck and circled the block returning to the exact same place in the alley.

He got out and walked slowly to the rear of the truck where he glanced down at my bumper sticker that reads 'Practice Random Acts of Kindness." He then got back into the truck and took out a pocketknife and very meticulously removed the plaque of Jesus, put it lovingly into his jacket pocket, left the car and walked off into the rain.

At 5:45 on the morning of January 23, our telephone rang and it was the police with the welcome information that they had found my truck. Where did they find it? Why, it was parked in an alley behind a building not ten minutes from where we live. They told me that if I could get there within the half an hour, I could drive it from the scene and save the expense of the tow fee. If I couldn't get there within that time they would have to tow it to the police impound yard. I thanked the officer on the phone and I left to get my truck right away.

On the way there I wondered how much damage my truck had sustained. Surely it had been stripped or trashed or both. Anything that could be sold like the spare tire, jack, tools and jumper cables would certainly be gone. But I was most pleasantly surprised to find my truck had been parked with care. It was neither stripped nor trashed. Everything was there, except my handwritten manuscript and music tapes. Hey, I was delighted just to get my truck back. When I started the truck, it was in perfect running order. I then thanked the police for their kindness and patience while waiting for me to get there. I drove back to my house and that's when I noticed that something was missing. The plaque of Jesus was not on the dashboard. It had been removed, just as I had seen it removed in my dream.

I started thinking about this and knowing how the Angels do their work, I hoped that if this young thief did indeed read my manuscript, what he found there would help him to get back on the right path and that maybe he would never steal again. I prayed that it be so.

In this little book I have told you the worst things that are going to happen, but it would take many volumes to tell you all the *wonderful* things that will be coming to us. These are beyond your wildest dreams. So rejoice and believe. There will be happiness in this world as we have never known, and when the smoke finally clears, at last the lion will lie down with the lamb.

I am now coming to the end of these pages. Angel Ruth will continue to give me messages from the other side and I will keep adding to this journal until it is published.

It was prophesied thousands of years ago that men would once again walk hand-in-hand with His angels. I believe this is that time. If you are ever sleeping on the dark side of night and you happen to be awakened by an annoying buzzing in your ear coupled with the sweet aroma of flowers, don't jump out of bed in fear. Just lie back, listen closely and enjoy the ride.

>>THE BEGINNING<<

AFTERWARD

Glenn Maxwell continues to receive messages from Angel Ruth. There will be another book written in the near future. It will be entitled, *Messages from Angel Ruth*.

I'm sure that after reading this book, many of you may want to contact Glenn to have Glenn ask questions of Angel Ruth. It has been made very clear that Angel Ruth is Glenn's Angel. She has been sent to him and only him to guide and assist. He still has jobs he has to do for God. Therefore, please do not ask questions of Angel Ruth.

However, if you think having contact with your angel is important, try rereading this book or buy another book on how to learn to contact your own angel. Your own angel can be of assistance in guiding you and there are even courses given on how to contact your angel.

Your angels always guide you, whether you are aware of it or not. Ever had a hunch? That is what is referred to as the "still, small voice inside you". When you do not pay attention to your intuition, you will find that going against it, usually is a mistake. The answers are always within us. Pay attention to that "still, small voice" inside you and you can't go wrong.

SUGGESTED READING TO
CONTACT YOUR ANGELS

The following books are the best books on the market for
getting in touch with your angels:

Books By TERRY LYNN TAYLOR:

    MESSENGERS OF LIGHT   -The angels' guide to
                                      Spiritual growth
    GUARDIANS OF HOPE   -The angels' guide to
                                        Spiritual growth
    THE ANGEL EXPERIENCE -Simple ways to
                                        cultivate the qualities
                                        qualities of the divine

Books by DOREEN VIRTUE, Ph.D.:

  ANGEL THERAPY – Healing messages for every area
of your life
  DIVINE GUIDANCE – How to have a dialogue with
God and your guardian angels

Book by ALMA DANIEL, TIMOTHY WYLLIE, and
ANDREW RAMER:

  ASK YOUR ANGELS –
A practical guide to working with the messengers of
Heaven to empower your life.

Book by JOHN RANDOLPH PRICE:
  Angel Energy